CONCILIUM

CONCILIUM
ADVISORY COMMITTEE

Gregory Baum	Montreal/QC. Canada
José Oscar Beozzo	São Paulo, SP Brazil
Wim Beuken	Louvain, Belgium
Leonardo Boff	Petrópolis, Brazil
John Coleman	Los Angeles, CA. USA
Norbert Greinacher	Tübingen, Germany
Gustavo Gutiérrez	Lima, Peru
Hermann Häring	Tübingen, Germany
Werner G. Jeanrond	Oslo, Norway
Jean-Pierre Jossua	Paris, France
Maureen Junker-Kenny	Dublin, Ireland
François Kabasele Lumbala	Kinshasa, Rep. Dem. Congo
Nicholas Lash	Cambridge, UK
Mary-John Mananzan	Manila, The Philippines
Alberto Melloni	Reggio, Emilia Italy
Norbert Mette	Münster, Germany
Dietmar Mieth	Tübingen, Germany
Jürgen Moltmann	Tübingen, Germany
Teresa Okure	Port Harcourt, Nigeria
Aloysius Pieris	Kelaniya/Colombo, Sri Lanka
Giuseppe Ruggieri	Catania, Italy
Paul Schotsmans	Louvain, Belgium
Janet Martin Soskice	Cambridge, UK
Elsa Tamez	San José, Costa Rica
Christoph Theobald	Paris, France
David Tracy	Chicago, Ill. USA
Marciano Vidal	Madrid, Spain
Ellen van Wolde	Tilburg, The Netherlands
Johannes Zizioulas	Pergamo, Turkey
Regina Ammicht Quinn	Tübingen Germany
Hille Haker	Chicago, USA
Jon Sobrino	San Salvador, El Salvador
Luiz Carlos Susin	Porto Alegre, Brazil
Silvia Scatena	Bologna, Italy
Susan A. Ross	USA, Los Angeles
Solange Lefebvre	Montreal/QC. Canada
Erik Borgman	Amsterdam, Netherlands
Andres Torres Queiruga	Santiago, Spain

CONCILIUM 2020/5

Differently Able:
For a Church Where All Belong

Edited by

Margareta Grüber,
Huang Po-Ho, Gianluca Montaldi

Published in 2020 by SCM Press, 3rd Floor, Invicta House, 108–114 Golden Lane, London EC1Y 0TG.

SCM Press is an imprint of Hymns Ancient & Modern Ltd (a registered charity) 13A Hellesdon Park Road, Norwich NR6 5DR, UK

Copyright © International Association of Conciliar Theology, Madras (India)

www.concilium.in

English translations copyright © 2020 Hymns Ancient & Modern Ltd.

All rights reserved. No part of this publication may be reproduced, stored in a retrieval system, or transmitted, in any form or by any means, electronic, mechanical, photocopying or otherwise, without the prior written permission of the Board of Directors of Concilium.

ISBN 978-0-334-05960-8

Concilium is published in March, June, August, October, December

Contents

Editorial   7

Part One: Introduction

Theology and Disability Studies:
A Bereft Reappraisal   13
Hans S. Reinders

Part Two: Reading Our Traditions

Catechesis For People With Disabilities:
A Look at the Path of the Catholic Church in Italy   29
VERONICA AMATA DONATELLO

Unbalanced Reading:
Dis/ability-Critical Approaches to Biblical Healing Narratives
Illustrated by Mk 7.31-37   37
MARKUS SCHIEFER FERRARI

Approaching Disability:
Pastoral History and Practice Analyzed Through the Models
of the Church   48
LUCA BADETTI

Rebuilding Christian Mission from the Perspective of
"Discriminated Differently Abled"   58
HUANG, PO HO

Part Three: Rethinking Humanity

Rethinking Charity   69
ANNE MASTERS

Living Together in the Household of God:
A Perspective from a Person with Disabilities 80
STEPHEN ARULAMPALAM

Towards Disability Theology in Christianity and Islam 90
NAEIMEH POURMOHAMMADI

Disability and Perfection 101
BERNHARD NITSCHE

Part Four: Reforming the Church

History and Comments of EDAN at the WCC 113
SAMUEL GEORGE

'Finding Something for Bénédicte to Do':
What Place can Women with Learning Difficulties Have in the
Eucharistic Liturgy? 118
TALITHA COOREMAN-GUITTIN

Liturgical Imagination at Full Stretch:
Possibilities for Leadership of Disabled People 128
MIRIAM SPIES

Relationships of Solidarity as Heterotopias Bringing Wholeness
to People with (and without) Disabilities 138
MARTIN M. LINTNER

Part Five: Theological Forum

Sacraments for a Sick World:
Thoughts on Sacramental Lockdown During the Pandemic 149
MARGARETA GRUBER

Contributors 155

Editorial

As soon as we ask what is disability, and even more when we want to define a disabled person, many difficulties arise: regardless of the distinction between physical and mental, when is an impediment or dysfunction transformed into a disability that characterizes the existence of a person? Is a (missing or deficient) function of the body to be decisive here? Since "my" body is essentially finished, what really limits my existence and my body? Disability, if we want go on using this word, depends from age, situation, family, and affects all levels of human existence: body, mind, learning, behaviour... and religion.

The ground of this reflection is therefore anthropology: indeed, religions' anthropologies could help or deny the identity of persons. From the point of view of critical theology, it is important first of all to analyse what in the history of thought has differentiated the 'different' or, more directly, which have been and continue to be the conditions that exclude from the common good people who do not want or can not be assimilated or "normalized". Among these assumptions, there are also positions of various religions and, in particular, the perception that Christianity has had and still has of diseases and limitations as consequences of a history of sin. These and similar positions give positive sanction to and helps to configure the pre-religious fear of diversity: from here, they contribute to creating the figure of the 'monster', of the 'witch', of the 'unfortunate' (literally, without grace) who are to hide, to let disappear. Above all, in modern liberal and consumerist society, a certain spirituality and a certain theology also give the risk of blessing the ideal of a human body and existence according to the canons of an (an)aestheticizing perfection that only creates further suffering.

On the contrary, reforming the Church is building a church as hospitality. In this question, it is about getting voice to the positive experiences that are resilient to any form of normalization of the different. We think, however, that it is also important to give a voice to the families and to

Editorial

the people who live their lives accompanied by a stable impairment. Too often, non-disabled people prejudice this discourse. Giving voice to others would perhaps be instructive and certainly less paternalistic; it can help theology to rethink in depth its anthropology and its vision of the church. After all, sin means rebelling against the fact that the limit constitutes the centre of the garden (D. Bonhoeffer), that diversity and identity contribute together to human maturity, that the value of a person is the ability to share the weakness of our created being, that is grace. De facto, when we think about different abilities we are thinking about questions of power and asking for the capability to empower people.

Articles are divided into four parts. The introductory part contains only the text of H.S. Reinders. We asked him to present the theology of disability as such. It highlights the tension that studies on disability have created within theology. The second part offers a critical reading of our traditions: from the point of view of catechesis and education (Veronica A. Donatello), of biblical hermeneutics (Markus Schiefer Ferrari), of systematic theology (Luca Badetti), and of the understanding of church (Po-Ho Huang). Starting on the side of disabled people offers new possibilities for reflection. Rethinking humanity is the task of the third part. It is about reviewing our ideas of what it means to be human and what the task of his story is (Bernhard Nitsche). For example, rethinking the charitable model can also contribute to improving the path for the defence of the rights of people with disabilities starting from our common dignity (Anne Masters) and from our living in solidarity and compassion a common house (Stephen Arulampalam). From this point of view, Christian theology can offer a model even outside its own tradition (Naeimeh Pourmohammadi). The fourth part offers some provocations to continue theological reflection. A brief commentary on the work done in the WCC in the meantime (Samuel George) helps to focus on what is already being done worldwide. Two contributions take as a starting point the position of disabled people in the liturgy (Talitha Cooreman-Guittin) and in the ministry (Miriam Spies), two sensitive areas that often reveal themselves as moments where the various speeches can receive their own falsification. Our program ends with a look into the heterotopia of places where the good face of solidarity can be shown and which we are ensured by the hope of being healed in our wounds (Martin Lintner).

Editorial

Whilst thinking and building this volume of *Concilium* two facts particularly affected us. The first concerns news relating to the abuses committed by Jean Vanier. Although these crimes were carried out by him on adult and non-disabled women, his figure certainly remains scarred and his writings and thoughts acquire a completely unpleasant light: as this volume testifies, we cannot act in watertight compartments, but the intersectionality of the problems forces us to have a critical look that points to the structural transformation of the problem. We must recognize the merit of L'Arche for having had the courage of an independent and transparent investigation of what happened.[1] The second stumbling block was the pandemic that hit the whole world so hard and undermined it as a whole. We have felt impaired in our potential and much of humanity is still in this situation. We have lived relegated, cut off from decisions, impeded in movement and observed on sight. Normality has become oddity, or perhaps we have only seen more clearly than ever those barriers and divisions that the so-called normality is capable to set. The egoity of the rich world has seen the violence of its societies turn against itself. This does not allow us to relativize the issue of disability, but affirming that this is an expression of the violence of modern society: the state of exception (G. Agamben) has revealed its globalizing power. The church is not unscathed from it.

Margareta Gruber, Po-Ho Huang, Gianluca Montaldi

Note

1. See http://www.arche-france.org/larche-annonce-resultats-lenquete-sur-son-fondateur [last visited on 25/06/2020].

Part One: Introduction

Theology and Disability Studies: A Bereft Reappraisal

HANS S. REINDERS

Reflecting on disability studies from the perspective of Christian theology is a daunting task, not only because disability studies as such has dethroned theological views, but also because an attempt to turn the tables is fraught with difficulty. Two main approaches to this problematic relationship will be discussed here. One starts from the mainstream view in disability studies to identify theological reflection with the 'charity' model of disability that regards disability as some kind of tragedy that requires a beneficent, embracing response from Christians to people who are to be pitied. The second approach pursues an opposite trajectory, in which theology is reinstalled as a 'master narrative' that provides the tools for scrutinizing the social theory underlying inquiries within disability studies. Given their methodological presuppositions, this second approach is strongly oriented towards Christian witness to account for its truth-claims. A generation of emerging scholars including many women, is engaging in academic work to renew this field of study.

I Introduction

Reflecting on disability studies from the perspective of Christian theology is a daunting task, and this for more than one reason. Not only because disability studies as such has dethroned theological views, but also because an attempt to turn the tables is fraught with difficulty. The narrative I am about to present is concerned with the tensions between the two in a way that can hardly be regarded other than as troublesome, particularly for those who have taken responsibility for serious theological reflection in this area. Two main approaches to this problematic relationship will be discussed here. One starts from the mainstream view in disability studies to identify theological reflection with the 'charity' model of disability that regards disability as some kind of tragedy that requires a beneficent, embracing response from Christians to people who are to be pitied.¹ In looking closer at this approach we will see that it subordinates theology to some version of a 'critical' social theory. Before it is allowed to speak theology needs to be cleared from the negative tone of traditional religious views on disability. The second approach pursues an opposite trajectory, in which theology is reinstalled as a 'master narrative' that provides the tools for scrutinizing the social theory underlying inquiries within disability studies. Theologians drawn towards this approach do not devote their attention primarily to the critical analysis of discrimination and rejection and the alternative project of inclusion and equal citizenship. Instead they develop a theological account of valuing disability centring on notions of 'friendship' and 'belonging'. It is not by accident, however, that their reflections are mostly concerned with the lives of persons with intellectual and developmental disabilities. Given their methodological presuppositions, this second approach is strongly oriented towards Christian witness to account for its truth-claims. This approach has only very recently received a terrible blow. The key witness in much of their work has been the theory and practice of L'Arche communities and its founder Jean Vanier.

II Eiesland's Ground Breaking Work

One way to characterize the first approach is to say that disability studies frames the legitimacy of theology. When it comes to theological reflection on disability studies, the reality of 'disability theology' is that it has its perspective shaped the other way around.² Many of the authors in this field have taken their point of departure in Nancy Eiesland's ground breaking work *The Disabled God*.³ As her subtitle suggests, Eiesland's thought was rooted in the tradition of liberation theology. Decisive for her methodology was to adopt the world of disability advocacy as her vantage point, not unlike the identification of liberation theologians with the plight of the poor and oppressed. In this move one recognizes the tradition of liberation theology as established in Clodovis Boff's *Theology and Praxis*.⁴ Theological reflection on the poor and oppressed ought to start from a critical social theory, if it is not to merely reproduce existing power relations of social and economic inequality. A similar methodology has been pursued by feminist theology in reflecting on the position of women in church and society.

Reflecting on her experience within the disability rights movement Eiesland pursued her task in a similar way, for which she used the 'minority group model' as a theoretical tool.⁵ Like many liberation theologians before her, that is to say, she approached the task of theological reflection from the outside in. In other words, the church and its theology appear as objects of change, not as its initiators.⁶ Her theology starts with insights obtained from critical theory. In what later came to be known as 'disability theology' we find similar moves. Authors in that field frequently adopt a perspective of disability advocacy to define the task of theological reflection.⁷ The world of disability experience is rewarded an epistemological privilege not unlike how Latin American liberation theology does with regard to the experience of 'the poor'.⁸ That experience is used as a lens through which the light of the Gospel shines more clearly. If God has a preference for the poor, listening to their experience will bring us closer to God's message for the world. In Eiesland's book similar moves are found, even when she does not use the same language. Persons with disabilities are reclaiming the truth of the Christian symbols, which means that the deity is not revealed as the triumphant God of ableism, but as the disabled God who is known by the stigmata of suffering. In Eiesland's words: the truth about God is part of the 'hidden history' of persons with disability as rejected and excluded people.⁹

III Turning Away From 'Religion'

The second reason why looking at disability studies from the perspective of theology is challenging, is different but closely connected. 'Religion' used to have a bad reputation in circles of disability advocates. Also in this regard Eiesland's book is a signpost. She wrote her book against the background of her experience in the church of her youth as a person with a disability. At best, the religious views she was familiar with promoted spiritual healing as a way of overcoming disability as a 'tragedy'. At worst, such views would not allow the notion of tragedy and saw all things happening in the world as according to God's will, which usually resulted in naming disability a consequence of 'sin'. In this respect quite a large number of our fellow Christians seem prepared to simply repeat the question addressed to Jesus by his disciples: 'Who sinned that this person is born disabled?' (John 9:2)[10] The tendency of regarding their disability, or that of their child, as some kind of 'evil' often seemed to be strengthened rather than attenuated in religious contexts. Many people who have sought redemption from their hardships in the religious community of their upbringing have found reason to doubt their religious beliefs. While most, if not all theologians working in this area have opposed this tendency, it is far from clear that the same can be said of many religious communities 'out there'. Too often one hears from families of persons with a disability finding themselves confronted by the view that there must be something wrong, why would they otherwise have 'to suffer such an ordeal'?[11]

In view of this landscape it can certainly be argued that it has significantly changed over the last decades. After all, who has not heard of the 'social' model of disability, indicating the social, economic, and cultural aspects of living with a disability that cannot be reduced to its biological condition? In a number of countries this awareness has led to the adoption of legislation seeking to promote equal citizenship for persons with disabilities. Speaking more generally, the adoption of the *Convention of the Rights of Persons with Disabilities* by the United Nations in 2006 suggests that traditional religious misconceptions of disability are losing ground in most parts of the globe. Perhaps they do. If so, one may maybe infer that the expanding critical work in religion and disability apparently has had some effect. However, fortunate as this conclusion would be, it does not by itself reopen the space for a conversation on disability and religion. Having experienced the negative impact of religion people may have not find themselves inclined to return to this conversation. Particularly not when, as a popular saying goes, bars, theatres and restaurants are frequently still more accessible than churches. In view of this alleged fact, what positive reason there can be to reflect theologically on disability studies?

One apparent reason is that the 'religious' question does not seem to go away. Over the years there has been a growing agreement among disability studies scholars that the separation between social and physical aspects of disability that constituted the classical version of the 'social model' in the work of scholars like Mike Oliver,[12] is untenable. The disabled body, exhausted, painful, inefficient, non-cooperative, whatever the case may be, matters. At any rate, the way persons with disabilities experience their bodies cannot be declared *anathema* – as the social model originally had it – without betraying the moral to inclusive supports. After all, the body is part of who the person with a disability is.[13]

In other words, there is no point in denying the eventual problems persons with disabilities and their families face in living with a 'defective' body. Acknowledging this is not a way to succumb to the power of ableism. It does not at all follow that the person with a disability is a problem to be solved. But there is no point in denying the harmful and painful aspects attached to disability, which means that at the fringes of disability experience the question of meaning reappears. The experience of vulnerability has never failed to raise questions regarding human finitude, and so does – eventually – the experience of disability. In Gaventa's words, the worlds of disability and spirituality are inevitably intertwined, *"Each leads to the other"*.[14] His study is directed against the tendency to privatize the question of meaning, as if that question had no place in thinking about adequate supports for persons with disabilities and their families. It indicates that with turning away from religion disability studies have also gone away from the question of meaning, and – by extension – also from theological reflection on this aspect of disability experience. There is no meaning in disability, scholars in critical disability studies would say, other than that one has to live with it as well as one possibly can.[15] And the rest is politics.

Striking in this connection, however, is testimony in the work of authors with first-hand experience of disability that points in a different direction. Nancy Eiesland would herself be the first to quote. While in her work she expressed her commitment to the cause of the disability rights movement, she also confessed that it failed to respond to her spiritual needs, as addressed in the question, "What does my disability mean?"[16]

Similarly Arne Fritzon, a Swedish theologian with cerebral palsy and a member of the Ecumenical Disability Advocates Network (EDAN), wrote on that same question in an essay with the title "Disability and Meaning."[17] Together with Samuel Kabue from Kenya, Fritzon was one of the authors of the document *A Church of All and for All*, issued by the World Council of Churches in 2003, in which they argued that *"those disabled people who share a Christian faith . . . have relied upon certain theological tools to address their existential need to explain the mystery and paradox of love and suffering, coexisting and giving meaning to their lives."*[18] This document further states:

In our wrestling with God, as disabled people we all ask the same basic questions, but the theological enquiry involved may be complex. Why me, or my loved one? Is there a purpose to my disability? The answers to those questions can be influenced by the expected time-span of a disability, and by the time and circumstances of its onset.[19]

Here we find testimony from persons with disabilities of a spiritual need to come to terms with their disability. So there is one apparent reason to return to theological reflection in thinking about disability, and that is the 'existential' aspect of disability experience. To suggest that questions about meaning are nothing but the betrayal of a lingering ableism reflects the same tendency towards reductionism that all 'nothing but' arguments about religion since the 19th century have been guilty of.

In the meantime the above argument does no more than represent a modest position. Many people in modern society continue to adhere to religious beliefs and some of these are persons with disabilities. There can be nothing wrong in accommodating them in their spiritual needs. One could even argue that it is part of a 'person-driven' supports system to allow for the possibility that also these needs are addressed.[20] But this can only mean, of course, that the relevance of theological reflection on disability experience solely depends on the presence of people for whom the question of meaning is real. Theological reflection on disability experience might have something useful to say, but only because there are service-users who indeed believe it may have something useful to say. There is no interest in such reflection other than theirs. On a more positive note, one of the things to be gained from critical disability studies is the recognition that persons with disabilities differ among each other in the same degree that people in all other segments of society differ from one another. What disability is, is one thing; what my disability means to me, is something very different. To the extent that disability experience is seen as framed by personal identity and vice versa, the legitimacy of addressing questions of meaning is beyond dispute.

IV The Subordination of Theology

Recognizing the connection between theological reflection on disability and the privatization of religious concerns, however, opens the avenue towards the second approach mentioned in the Introduction. This is the approach that rejects the subordination of theology to social theory, and claims that reflecting on the Christian faith can produce irreducible insights into the reality of disability experience, irreducible in the sense that they cannot be obtained otherwise. In other words, it contests that theology is rightly dethroned. To be able to present this second approach, it will be a useful steppingstone to look at an exemplary article on the primacy of disability studies named The Disability Studies Paradigm by David Pfeiffer that was published in an anthology entitled Rethinking Disability.[21] Affirming that disability studies nowadays is a well-established discipline in Academia, Pfeiffer's basic claim is that "Its fundamental paradigm must be understood in order to grasp the implications of disability studies and utilize the knowledge produced by it."[22] This means that anything important that can be known about disability will be produced within this paradigm. With this claim Pfeiffer commits himself to a hierarchical ordering of knowledge. To get a true understanding of this fundamental paradigm the author proposes to look at several other 'models' of disability, one of which is a popular religious view that connects disability to sin. This is how he characterizes this view: "The popular view is that disability comes from sinful activity because God would not allow such a terrible thing to happen to good people."[23] Pfeiffer traces this view to originate in the cultural phenomenon of a deep-seated fear of difference.

The search for an explanation of what is different and feared then becomes the need to find blame for what happened. The explanation for why one person becomes disabled and another person does not is too often found in the concept of sin."[24]

Pfeiffer wants to argue that many people do no longer hold this religious view inasmuch that it expresses "a demand for a causal explanation where none exists that will satisfy the seeker."[25] The notion of sin as a placebo for seeking answers were none exist. But people persist nonetheless in fearing disability, which is why they consider persons with disabilities as objects of pity. Or else, when such negative perceptions are rejected, they are admired or their strength, and heralded as inspirational figures.[26]

At the root of all these responses, Pfeiffer argues, is the same notion that underscores the religious view. Disability is something that needs to be overcome and, as such, it better did not exist. Pfeiffer disagrees with a key to the disability studies paradigm. "Most of these views have their beginnings in the fear of disability, but disability is a part of human life."[27]

What makes the argument adduced here exemplary is the categorical denial of an explanation for the occurrence of disability that is not rooted in the disability studies paradigm. No explanation for the occurrence of disability can be found, it is claimed, because "none exists". This categorical denial means that the premise of Pfeiffer's argument cannot be the result of scientific investigations. While this claim does reflect the disability studies paradigm as 'fundamental', at the same time it suggests a rival conception of theology. It presupposes a conception of the universe as a space for the occurrence of randomly distributed events, which is a conception that cannot be obtained from disability studies as an academic discipline. What happens is that the popular view of seeing a link between disability and sin is in fact overruled and outlawed rather than refuted by the disability studies paradigm. While I have no stake whatsoever in defended that link, I do want to say that only arguments produced by theological reflection can in fact show why 'sin' is not a concept that in any way is helpful in explaining disability. The paradigm of disability studies can overrule popular religious views, denounce and marginalize them, but it cannot as a matter of fact produce arguments rebutting them without presenting itself as a rival conception of theology.[28]

V On Being Unapologetically Theological

The second approach to theological reflection on disability may characterized as the attempt to reinstall theology as a primary discourse. This approach can be best illuminated by contrasting David Pfeiffer's postulate of the disability studies paradigm as fundamental with John Milbank's argument in Theology and Social Theory.[29] According to Milbank the subordination of theology disguises the overtaking of a single aspect of social reality by enthroning its primacy over all other aspects. The unmasking of religion by the great masters of suspicion in the 19th century – Marx, Nietzsche, and Freud – is achieved only by elevating other aspects of social reality than religion to a superior position, thereby installing the social theory that produces this move in the position of a rival 'master-narrative'.[30]

Theological reflections on disability mirroring this second approach may not follow Milbank's radical orthodoxy in all of its intellectual grandeur and ramification, but it is not hard to trace familiar inclinations. A clear example would be John Swinton's *Becoming Friends of Time*, in which he uses the phenomenology of disability experience – especially as mediated by learning disabilities – as a topos to criticize secular notions of time for being oblivious of the creatureliness of human existence.[31] Another example would be my own book Receiving the Gift of Friendship,[32] which is arguing that non-theological accounts of the humanity of persons with profound intellectual disabilities are doomed to fail. They necessarily depend on substantial criteria for a human self that such persons inevitably must fail to meet. Arguing constructively for the recognition of a self that is rooted in God's action it seeks to overcome the categorization of human being that puts persons with profound disability in secular thought unavoidably at risk as human beings of a lesser kind.

Following Milbank's account of theology reasserting itself as a 'master-narrative' it should not be missed that theologians attracted to this approach have repudiated any form of foundational epistemology. 'Master-narrative' is rhetorical. What has dethroned theology is precisely the Kantian project of establishing the philosophical foundation of 'pure' reason as the tribunal before which all other claims to knowledge have to account for themselves. The inevitable result of Kant's project was religion within the limits of reason alone. While 19th century liberal theology attempted to hold its ground by arguing for the quest for meaning as the essence of purified religion – implying a conception of humanity that would render persons with intellectual disabilities anyhow as 'subhuman' – that option is no longer open to their contemporary heirs. No independent criteria to establish the truth of any knowledge claims are available. There is no epistemological position that is not a position, to put it in Hauerwassian terms.

On this view Christian theology has only one option left. Theological claims can only be established as true by showing how they become real. This has direct implications for theological reflection on disability. Christian claims to how the love of God extends to all human beings regardless of their state or condition can only be demonstrated by witness. It is not by accident, then, that theologians inclined to follow Milbank's project of reinstalling theology in its own right, have found their prime witness in the communities of L'Arche. These are communities where persons with an without intellectual disabilities try to live according to the Gospel. More in particular, their theological convictions could not but lead to embracing the life and work of its founder Jean Vanier, independent of any subordination of theology to critical social theory. The connections are clearly identifiable in the work of theologians such as Hauerwas, Swinton, and myself.[33] Their non-foundational epistemologies led them to redefine 'truth' as 'truthfulness' and refer to Vanier as their key-witness. Christian accounts of communal life together with human beings with disabilities, profound or otherwise, were proven true because of the truthfulness of Jean Vanier and his people as, in his own words, a followers of Jesus.[34]

Well, it turns out we have wilfully been misled, precisely at the point where it is most critical. Perhaps the truth of what Vanier taught can be argued by theologians on grounds of Christology or pneumatology with some plausibility, but it cannot be demonstrated by the truthfulness of his life. He has been uncovered as a key-member of a group of people who for many years were engaged in dubious sexual relationships, some of which relationships depended on unequal spiritual power and were therefore abusive. There is a time to lament the women who suffered the consequences of being trapped in abusive relationships. After that, there is time to rethink whether and how the truthfulness of L'Arche communities can be maintained now that its great leader has fallen.

VI In Conclusion

The two approaches to theological reflection on disability studies I have described here do not represent blue prints. Many other works could have been listed showing hybrid variations of theological positions somewhere in between the two opposites. Not many theologians who are working, or have been working in the field would deny that they have learned much from their colleagues in disability studies, but it is not evidently the case that the reverse is also true. The resulting picture of where we now are appears somewhat uncertain and indeterminate, which is to some extent a reflection of the over-representation of western, male and white academics in the field of disability theology. A generation of emerging scholars including many women, is engaging in academic work. A number of them frequently met since 2010 at the annual meetings of SITD (Summer Institute of Theology and Disability). A wider circle occasionally met in their contributions to the Journal of Disability and Religion (formerly as the Journal of Religion, Disability, and Health), and other fora for publishing their work. For those working in Europe, the dwindling position of established religion means that engaging in a marginal academic field concerned with the lives of marginalized people requires an act of courage. For others, mostly working in North-America, reclaiming theology against the subordination by other disciplines the task of future orientations 'after Vanier' appears inevitable. Given this changing landscape, the emerging mixture of new voices will bring about that in ten years from now the picture will most likely be a very different one. Introducing theological reflections on disability studies will at that time no doubt result in an equally different story.

Notes

1. William C. Gaventa, Disability and Spirituality. Recovering Wholeness. Waco TX: Baylor UP, 2018, pp. 26-28.
2. The emerging field of disability theology is much broader than I will be able to address here. Among the most quoted works are John Swinton, *Resurrecting the Person: Friendship and the Care of People with Mental Health Problems.* Nashville TN: Abingdon, 2000; Amos Yong, *Theology and Down Syndrome: Reimagining Disability in Late Modernity.* Waco TX: Baylor UP, 2007; Thomas E. Reynolds, *Vulnerable Communion: A Theology of Disability and Hospitality.* Grand Rapids MI: Brazos, 2008; Hans S. Reinders, *Receiving the Gift of Friendship, Profound Disability, Theological Anthropology, and Ethics.* Grand Rapids MI: Eerdmans, 2008; Deborah Beth Creamer. *Disability and Christian Theology. Embodied Limits and Constructive Possibilities.* Oxford: Oxford UP, 2009; In general most of the works published in *Studies in Religion, Theology, and Disability* (published by Baylor University Press) have been seminal to the field.
3. Nancy L. Eiesland, *The Disabled God: Toward a Liberatory Theology of Disability.* Nashville, TN: Abingdon, 1994.
4. Clodovis Boff, *Theology and Praxis: Epistemological Foundations.* Maryknoll, NY: Orbis, 1987. I presented an analysis of Boff's book in my dissertation *Violence, Victims, and Rights.* Vrije Universiteit Amsterdam, 1988.
5. See Eiesland, *The Disabled God*, p. 24.
6. Reinders, *Receiving the Gift of Friendship*, p. 170.
7. A good example is Beth Creamer's *Disability and Christian Theology.*

8. See Phillip Berryman, *Liberation Theology*. Philadelphia: Temple UP, 1987; Joy Gordon, Liberation theology as critical theory: The notion of the 'privileged' perspective'. *Philosophy & Social Criticism*. Vol. 22, 5 (1996), pp. 85-102; Scot Danforth, Liberation theology of disability and the option for the poor. *Disability Studies Quarterly*. Vol. 25, 3 (2005), https://dsq-sds.org/article/view/572/749.
9. Reinders, *Receiving the Gift of Friendship*, p. 171.
10. For an extended reading of the story withdrawing from the miracle of healing and focusing on the man's recognizing Jesus as the 'son of man' see Reinders, *Receiving the Gift of Friendship*, p. 322-329.
11. Hans S. Reinders, *Disability, Providence, and Ethics: Bridging Gaps, Transforming Lives*. Waco: Baylor, 2014. A quick and dirty search for accounts of religious views connecting disability and sin on Google has more than 60 million hits, which at any rate suggests the notion is not dead at all, nor is it specific for any particular religion. It also brings up a wealth of publications. Just to name two among many other possible examples: Pauline A. Otieno, Biblical and Theological Perspectives on Disability: Implications on the Rights of Persons with Disability in Kenya. *Disability Studies Quarterly*. Vol. 29, 4 (2009), https://dsq-sds.org/article/view/988/1164; Mikel Burley, Retributive Karma and the Problem of Blaming the Victim. *International Journal for Philosophy of Religion*. Vol. 74, 2 (2012), pp. 149–165.
12. Michael Oliver, *Understanding disability: from theory to practice*. Basingstoke: Macmillan, 1996.
13. See for example Tom Shakespeare and Nicholas Watson, The social model of disability: An outdated ideology? *Research in Social Science and Disability*. Vol. 2 (2002), pp. 9-28.
14. Gaventa, *Disability and Spirituality*, p.9.
15. Hans S. Reinders, Is there meaning in disability? Or is it the wrong question? *Journal of Religion, Disability & Health*. Vol. 15, 1 (2011), pp. 57-71.
16. Nancy Eiesland, Liberation, Inclusion, and Justice: A Faith Response to Persons with Disabilities. In *Impact: Feature Issue on Faith Communities and Persons with Developmental Disabilities*. Vol. 14, 3 (2001), pp. 2–3.
17. Arne Fritzon, Disability and Meaning. In Arne Fritzon and Samuel Kabue, *Interpreting Disability: A Church for All*. Geneva: WCC, 2003, pp. 1–23.
18. World Council of Churches, *A Church of All and for All: An Interim Statement*. Geneva: WCC, 2003, p. 3.
19. Ibid.
20. It turns out that in some western countries it is not allowed to offer supports for spiritual needs because support systems as such are monitored by public authorities who consider 'religious' or 'spiritual' questions to belong to the realm of the private.
21. David Pfeiffer, The Disability Studies Paradigm. In Patrick Devlieger, Frank Rusch, and David Pfeiffer, *Rethinking Disability. The Emergence of New Definitions, Concepts, and Communities*. Antwerp: Garant, 2003, 95-100.
22. Pfeiffer, Disability Studies Paradigm, p. 97. It should be noted from the start that Pfeiffer's account presents the emergence of the new paradigm in the US.
23. Pfeiffer, Disability Studies Paradigm, p. 98.
24. Ibid.
25. Ibid.
26. Ibid.
27. Ibid.
28. Of course it will be noticed, in this connection, that Pfeiffer overstates his case because

disability is perfectly explicable in terms of its causes by reference to the natural sciences, at least to some extent. Disability has at any rate something to do with occurrences in the human body, without which the very notion would fail to make sense in the first place. In can certainly be denied, as presumably disability studies scholars like Pfeiffer are inclined to do, that knowledge of disabilities produced in the sciences – medicine, genetics, molecular biology – is in any way definitive of what disability *is*. But again, that assertion can only be warranted by the subordination of knowledge from the sciences to the knowledge produced by disability studies. This shows what it means to assert a 'fundamental' paradigm.

29. A. J. Milbank, *Theology and Social Theory. Beyond Secular Reason*. Oxford: Blackwell, 1989.

30. Milbank, *Theology and Social Theory*, p. 52. See Gordon E. Michalson, Re-Reading the Post-Kantian Tradition with Milbank. *The Journal of Religious Ethics.* Vol 32, 2 (2004), pp. 357-383, p.358; also Richard H. Roberts, Transcendental Sociology? A Critique of John Milbank's Theology and Social Theory. Beyond Secular Reason. *Scottish Journal of Theology.* Vol. 46, 4 (1993), pp. 527-535.

31. John Swinton, *Becoming Friends of Time: Disability, Timefullness, and Gentle Discipleship.* London: SCM, 2017.

32. Reinders, *Receiving the Gift of Friendship*, p. 11, 15, pp. 273-275.

33. From the many publications that could be listed here, I mention Stanley M. Hauerwas, Timeful Friends: Living with the Handicapped. In Stanley Hauerwas, *Sanctify Them in the Truth: Holiness Exemplified*. Edinburgh: T&T Clark, 1998, pp. 143-156; John Swinton (ed.), *Living Gently in a Violent World: The Prophetic Witness of Weakness*. Downers Grove IL: Intervarsity, 2008; Hans S. Reinders, Transforming Friendship: An Essay in Honour of Jean Vanier. *Journal of Disability and Religion*. Vol. 19, 4 (2015), pp. 340-364.

34. Interview with Jean Vanier: 'To be a Christian is to love people who are different.' Premier Christianity – June 2015 (https://www.premierchristianity.com/Past-Issues/2015/June-2015).

Part Two: Rethinking Our Traditions

Catechesis For People With Disabilities: A Look at the Path of the Catholic Church in Italy

VERONICA AMATA DONATELLO

The education in faith of the baptised by a united process of human-Christian maturation is a journey which does not take place automatically but which requires educational action, a mediation of personal and community growth and maturing addressed to all. Catechesis is an essential part of it. This educational attention is addressed with particular care to *people with disabilities* (PwD). This article analyses the development of cultural progress in Italy which today results in a language of "person" with disabilities, the ecclesial consequences in the principal Italian catechetical documents and the characteristics of an "inclusive" catechesis, capable of valuing everyone without excluding anyone.

I The Context: the discussion about disabilities

The education in faith of the baptised by a joint process of human-Christian maturation is a journey which does not happen automatically but which requires educational action, a mediation of personal and community growth and maturing addressed to all. Catechesis is an essential part of it: within its evangelising mission it is considered "foremost in the educational role of the Church".[1]

This educational attention is addressed with particular care to *people with disabilities* (PwD). We will analyse the development of cultural progress in Italy which today results in a language of "person" with disabilities, the ecclesial consequences in the principal Italian catechetical documents and the characteristics of an "inclusive" catechesis, capable of valuing everyone without excluding anyone.

In recent years the manner in which the reality of disability is perceived has changed. Across Globally some billion PwD, in other words 15% of the world's population, have to face discrimination and obstacles, which reduce the right to participate in social life on equal terms with other citizens.[2]

The terms by which PwD have been defined in the past – from "handicapped, bearers of handicaps, disabled, disability, differently-abled, etc." –, have become part of daily use, both by experts and by those not involved in this work; and this significance of words becomes the mirror of social "representations" linked to PwD. Being seen as a person or non-person with the emphasis on deficiency leads to ambivalence about belonging to a community; while highlighting solely the deficiency re-establishes the image of a fragile subject,[3] different, lacking in ability, who needs medicalised approaches, forcing the PwD to feel "different" per se.

Scientific reflection, supported by the development of the concept of educability, is the challenge which has enabled seeing the PwD as a subject capable of learning and, therefore, of bringing about a change in perspective: a national and international cultural *humus* which stimulates a vision of the PwD not as a "lacking human being", but rather as a person equal to others.[4]

Over the last century, access to education, initially special education and then integrated, alongside the discovery of one's own role in social action, provided the PwD with new opportunities. Educational formation has particularly contributed to supporting this change of an epistemological nature.

The same theme of disability has been the object of studies which have developed important theoretical models giving rise to readings from different angles.[5] Above all, the *Capability* approach includes objectives such as fostering the wellbeing, justice and development of the PwD: the subject must be able to choose freely one option rather than another and, at the same time, society is tasked with offering accessible alternatives, eliminating or reducing the barriers.

The *Disability Studies* theoretical thread, developed primarily in North European and Anglo-American environments, is an inter-disciplinary research approach which analyses disability as a social, political and cultural phenomenon, and suggests a perspective which no longer interprets disability as an individual biological condition, but as a social construction, identifying those elements which "disable" the person.

The bio-psycho-social model of the ICF (International Classification of Functioning, Disability and Health) represents one of the most important contributions precisely because it allows a phenomenology of the human person in its entirety, enabling us to grasp its multi-dimensionality. According to this perspective the possibilities of including the PwD are not inversely proportionate to the gravity of the *deficiency*, but they refer as a priority to the variables of the environment, first of all the close environments of the family and of society, as well as through the analysis of the new DSM-5 (Diagnostic and Statistical Manual of Mental Health Disorders), which is of fundamental interest beyond the clinical and rehabilitation setting, since it clarifies and combines very clearly the revolutionary contribution of the ICF (International Classification of Functioning, Disability and Health) as an opportunity to observe and measure the functioning of the person in interaction with the environment of life and the context.

Considering the development towards PwD, the Church, too, while not favouring any one approach, feels the urgency for inclusion by implementing processes in the various spheres of life, because 'still today we can see the presence of the culture of waste and many of them feel that they exist without belonging and without participating'[6] in secular and Christian society.

Despite these new perspectives and approaches, the difficulties and prejudices which act along two parallel trajectories remain: on the one hand they influence the construction of "being person", because they create conditioning, and on the other they strongly influence the type of relation and relationship which is established between them, structuring a very distinctive *up-down* in the pastoral sphere, too.

Our country, in that sense, reveals itself to be "pioneering" in the international panorama as well as in the religious sphere. In recent years church praxis acted according to two approaches, both erroneous: one was committed to the "care" of people as a charitable act, while the other considered PwD as innocent "victim souls", predestined to suffer on behalf of others.[7] These prejudices offend PwD and remove responsibility from the Christian community to recognise them as *brothers and sisters* by virtue of Baptism and, therefore, not passive subjects of evangelization but co-builders of the Kingdom.

This reflection was born out of three concepts which marked the approach both of society and of the Church: *assimilation* through a charitable and helpful approach limited itself to introducing PwD into contexts separated from that person; *integration* guaranteed respect for formal rights in places, since "special" PwD necessitated special places and contributions; finally, *inclusion* prevails in all the international documents and those of the Magisterium too, where the PwD is considered a person, citizen with full rights. In fact, the presence of PwD obliges the community and its ecclesial bodies to re-think being Church, to journey towards an "inclusive pastoral care".

So it is urgent that we accept the need to work on the community context, an educational challenge for *Us* which demands carrying out pluri-directional and synodal communicative processes, processes which remove barriers / prejudices and promote responsiveness, participation.[8] It is essential to go from a community focussed on "pastoral survival" to the *We*, involving the family to create generating places which include the different dimensions of life, becoming *We the People of God*.

The theme of prejudice becomes an obstacle for a generative community and it often happens that the Church offers the PwD the possibility of existing, to make them a true part of the Church especially if they have received the Sacraments. This opens out to the discovery that attention on Christian initiation is not enough, because, as H. Arendt states, "we can know what they have but not what they are".[9] It is essential to weave a full relationship, which enables them to tell their story, to enable their own desires to emerge, and which is not exclusive of the so-called "normal".

The new vision which is outlined is that of a *Church of Us* as a *relational body* without boundaries, which does not reason on the basis of religious and social prejudice,[10] which does not exclude any minority, does not work in terms of welfare, but which becomes a collective experience of a constitutive pluralism where the *Church of Us* educates *Us*.

II The focus of catechesis on persons with disabilities

The post-conciliar period was prolific for Italian catechesis, via the Catechetical Project, which finds its generative nucleus in the 1970 *Fundamental Document*, along with the *Catechisms* of the Italian Episcopal Conference,[11] the Documents of the decades, the II Note on *Christian Initiation*[12] which states that for all disabled people it is possible to access the three sacraments because Baptism by its nature is ordained to chrismal completion and to the sacramental fullness which is reached in participation in the Eucharist, and the pastoral Guidelines *Incontriamo Gesù* and the specific documents from the catechesis and disability Department *Iniziazione Cristiana alle persone disabili. Orientamenti e proposte* (2004).[13] From the outset there was a focus on catechesis of the PwD.

From these documents emerge some supportive ideas: the subjectivity of the PwD, the plurality of languages, support for families as the evangelical task of the community, the formation which activates a synergy which accompanies the inclusive process in the communities. One grasps the prophetic ecclesial intuition about the concept of integration-inclusion, subject to the human-Christian recognition of the dignity of the PwD, the central role of the community in accepting and initiating processes of *empowerment*, and formation in teams, to use the "numerous languages".

The *Fundamental Document*, which anticipated the first Italian law on the inclusion of PwD, proposed a renewed vision of the Church, womb which generates life in Christ; in part III it emphasises the special attention for those who are less able, maladjusted and mentally handicapped.[14]

It highlighted in particular the importance of preparation of catechists for handing on the faith not in a reduced or infantile manner, synergy with the family through adapted language and the creation of a welcoming environment, so as to make possible participation in liturgical life and a testimonial form. It is evident that the key concept is collegiality: the whole community is the subject of catechesis by virtue of Baptism and there is no need for "special catechists". The inclusive strategies which are initiated are contained in the expression: «mentality of faith and faith-life integration»[15] in which there is no talk of method, it is not the taking of a stance, but it becomes a criterion of evaluative choice.[16]

45 years on from the *Fundamental Document*, 2014 saw the publication

of *Incontriamo Gesù. Orientamento per l'annuncio e la catechesi in Italia*,[17] where the word "disability" is never defined, suffice to make one think there has been an oversight. In truth, in this document there emerges the journey undertaken by the Church and the PwD themselves; a careful reading of the text leads to the realisation of the new panorama which the bishops are proposing to the whole ecclesial reality. The idea of the document is that of re-thinking catechesis in an "inclusive" perspective, where adherence to the ecclesial dimension is open to all, and so to PwD, too, a resource for it.

It is possible to trace this perspective in all four sections of the text: in the Christian anthropological vision; in the focus on formation of catechists which goes from sacramental preparation in a "special" perspective to an accompanying in faith; in a new vision of the educational action of catechesis and the proclamation of the faith by an accompanying throughout the span of life and in the various places of life; and in the full participation in the life of the community. The opportunity to offer support to parishes through methodologies and inclusive resources is highlighted, appreciating liturgical participation and harmonising ritual symbolic language.

III An inclusive catechesis

The Church has the responsibility to carry out the missionary mandate of Jesus: "Go, therefore, and make disciples of all nations" (*Matt* 28:19) and catechesis has always tried to realise this task from the perspective of service.

It is important for the Church "to feel involved in this field, not just on special and dedicated occasions, but in its ordinary life. It would be appropriate and important, therefore, that catechesis, with all its methods, styles and programmes, also heeded people with disabilities, not making anyone feel different, nor incapable of God's love".[18]

To ensure that catechesis possesses an identity which knows how to grasp the actual applications through the three tensions (*proposal, transmission, mission*), it is appropriate that PwD are participating involving the body and the senses, which are *portae fidei* for them. Often, PwD do not have a conceptual, hypothetical and deductive intelligence, their intellectual capacity remains in the concrete and hence it is important to appreciate the sensory channels and the body. It is essential to understand that for many of them catechesis, the Bible with logical inferences and metaphors, abstract thought, all become a struggle and they require other channels, which are not just the oral;[19] and therefore the support of images becomes essential to aid comprehension.

In this way we highlight the use of a multi-sided engaging pedagogy, illustrative are the biblical recitatives which use the force of the repetitiveness of the central biblical phrase combined with body movement, with the stereotypes and lallations of the PwD; and this catechetical mode is necessary for anyone who works for the completion of Christian initiation with disabled adults and / or comorbidities.

The richness of art, in its multiplicity of evocative potential is an excellent pastoral support for meetings of catechesis and liturgical participation. Furthermore, catechesis focussed on biblical narration, debunking the thought that only when one understands can one experience a true encounter with the Word, is effective in pastoral courses. People with neurodevelopmental disorders certainly have difficulties, but by knowing how to declare "the Word" with consideration and through strategies, its potential of *empowerment* emerges. The possibilities which the ICT offer for inclusion creating community are facilitators which enable the removal of the *text-support-environment* barrier.

Every person, with or without a disability, has a unique and specific vocation and therefore the Church has the same duties to PwD as it does to all the faithful. Furthermore, those who have not received Baptism also have the right to receive catechesis, since every person is called to salvation.[20]

In conclusion, our desire is that PwD can increasingly themselves become catechists in the community[21] and that this inclusive pastoral process, already underway in Italy, may spread in Churches throughout

Translated by Patricia Kelly

Notes

1. Second Vatican Council, Declaration on Christian Education *Gravissimum Educationi*, 28 October 1965, n. 4. Cfr. Enchiridion Vaticanum Vol. 1, Documenti ufficiali del Concilio

Vaticano II (1962-1965), Bologna: EDB, 1975, nn. 450-475, 459.
2. Cfr. Andrea Regimenti, *Caritas: più di un miliardo di persone vive nel mondo con qualche forma di disabilità*, in Agenzia Sir | Agensir.it, 3 December 2019 (Url: https://www.agensir.it/mondo/2019/12/03/caritas-piu-di-un-miliardo-di-persone-vive-nel-mondo-con-qualche-forma-di-disabilita/ *[02/06/2020]*).
3. Cfr. John Swinton, *Who is the God We Worship*, Journal of Pastoral Theology 14 (2011) 2, 278-281.
4. Antonello Mura, "Disabilità, identità e rappresentazioni sociali tra passato e presente", in Id. – Antioco Luigi Zurru (ed.), *Identità, soggettività e disabilità. Processi di emancipazione individuale e sociale*, Milan: FrancoAngeli, 2013, 30.
5. Rocco Di Santo, *Sociologia della disabilità. Teorie, modelli, attori e istituzioni*, Milan: FrancoAngeli, 2013.
6. Francis, Message for International Day of Persons with Disabilities, 3 December 2019.
7. Cfr. Justin Glyn, «*Noi*» *non* «*loro*». *La disabilità nella chiesa*, La Civiltà Cattolica, 2020, 1 (4/18 gennaio 2020), 41-52.
8. Serena Noceti, "Educare nella comunità cristiana, co-educarsi come comunità", in Pio Zuppa (ed.), *Apprendere nella comunità cristiana. Come dare "ecclesialità" alla catechesi oggi*, Leumann (TO): Elledici, 2012, 92.
9. Hannah Arendt citata da Charles Gardou, *Nessuna vita è minuscola. Per una società inclusiva*, Milan: Mondadori, 2015, 52.
10. Pierangelo Sequeri, *La pietà oggi fra pietismo ed egualitarismo*, Vita e Pensiero 2 (2016), 97-103.
11. In the publication of the *Catechisms* of the Italian Episcopal Conference there is no suggestion of separate support but the Note (see below) suggests educational strategies.
12. Cfr. Consiglio Episcopale Permanente, Nota pastorale *L'iniziazione cristiana: 2*, n. 58, in ECEI/6, n. 2117.
13. Ufficio Catechistico Nazionale, *Iniziazione Cristiana alle persone disabili. Orientamenti e proposte*, Bologna: EDB, 2004.
14. Conferenza Episcopale Italiana, *Il rinnovamento della catechesi*, nn. 125 e 127, ECEI/1, nn. 2746 e 2753, EDB, Bologna 1985.
15. *Ibidem*, nn. 38-39. Cfr. ECEI/1, nn. 2481-2487.
16. *Ibidem*, n. 52. Cfr. ECEI/1, nn. 2529-2530.
17. Cfr. Idem, *Incontriamo Gesù. Orientamenti per l'annuncio e la catechesi in Italia*, Bologna: EDB, 2014.
18. Francesco Spinelli – Eugene R. Sylva, "Conclusioni e prospettive", in Pontificio consiglio per la promozione della nuova evangelizzazione, *Catechesi e persone con disabilità. Un'attenzione necessaria nella vita quotidiana della Chiesa. Prospettive teologiche e pastorali*, Cinisello Balsamo (Mi): San Paolo, 2018, 207.
19. Sergio Melogno *et al.*, *Explaining Metaphors in High-Functioning Autism Spectrum Disorder Children: A brief Report*, Research in Austim Spectrum Disorders 6 (2012) 2, 683-689.
20. Cfr. Direttorio Generale per la catechesi, n. 189.
21. Francesco, Discorso in occasione del Convegno promosso dal Pontificio consiglio per la nuova evangelizzazione, 21 ottobre 2017.

Unbalanced Reading: Dis/ability-Critical Approaches to Biblical Healing Narratives Illustrated by Mk 7.31-37

MARKUS SCHIEFER FERRARI

As illustrated by the example of the healing of a deaf man with a speech impediment, in Mk 7.31-37, a comparison of traditional approaches to interpretation with a hermeneutics based on a dis/ability critique raises questions about the ideas of wholeness and visions of healing derived from biblical healing narratives. Drawing on so-called Dis/ability Studies produces an approach to interpretation that understands disability as a contingent, socio-cultural or historical construct that is very often created and passed on by forms of literary description. When the context of the biblical texts and that of today's readers are taken into account, in reading New Testament healing stories we find, amazingly, hope in the power of Jesus' miracles to change the world and the realisation that human fragility changes the interpretation of these narratives.

Interpreting New Testament healing miracles is both challenging and irritating because it involves not only questions about one's own sense of possibility and reality, but also and especially questions about ideas of normality and the images in which we imagine hope for ourselves and others. As the following example of the healing of a deaf man with a speech impediment in Mk 7.31-37 shows,[1] the emphases shift considerable according to the particular hermeneutical perspective, especially when, as with dis/ability-critical hermeneutics, the starting point is the vulnerability and fragility of the human person and this is contrasted with the perfectibility visions embodied in the healing narratives.

The story in Mark 7 on the one hand opens with confidence in healing and – with an allusion to Is 35.5-6 – visions of a future of wholeness in which 'the eyes of the blind shall be opened, and the ears of the deaf unstopped' (Mk 7.37), but on the other hand such images of hope today seem to us completely exclusive in terms of today's insistence on inclusion. This, for example, is the emphasis of Julia Watts Belser, a rabbi and professor of religious studies and Jewish studies at Washington's Georgetown University, who herself uses a wheelchair. She stresses that in 'Isaiah's vision of a renewed world' she greatly values the end of poverty, but is critical of 'the way he talks about disabilities'. Isaiah 35, she says, 'confronts us with the question of how we envisage the place of our body in the coming, future world,' and whether 'there is a place for disability in our hope for the future'. If there is a heaven, she would be 'very disappointed if heaven were not completely accessible'. For her, disability is 'not a disease, not suffering, not something bad', but part of her own identity, an everyday aspect of her own life. 'This is how I was created, this is the life I'm familiar with. It is sometimes complicated, it is sometimes frustrating, but it is also joyful, a source of imagination and creative. I can hardly imagine myself without disability. All I know I know through this body: my spirituality, my knowledge of God, my political awareness, my friendships and the groups I belong to, my intellectual work – my whole sense of myself is bound up with disability. I refuse to reject all this as though it were nothing.'[2]

This sort of unbalanced dis/ability-critical interpretation of biblical healing narratives therefore attempts to trace back concepts of hope and wholeness to their roots in diverse anthropological contexts of experience and to look behind familiar interpretation techniques, but is at the same time also aware of the fragility and limitations of its own exegetical and hermeneutical approach.[3]

I Rethinking Disability – hermeneutical consequences of Disability Studies

Before explaining various, often controversial approaches to the interpretation of Mk 7.31-37, I should like briefly to look at some core consideration of so-called Dis/ability Studies that lead to a different view, not only of disability, but also of the way it is represented, for example, in the New Testament.[4]

The concept of disability normally used and treated as obvious is by no means univocal, but is a dynamic concept heavily dependent on its particular cultural and temporal context. Using the category of 'disability' as a collective concept for a whole variety of physical, mental, spiritual or sensory limitations is probably a product of bourgeois society since the Enlightenment and so cannot be simply transferred to the ancient world, which had no similar overarching concept. From the perspective of Dis/ability Studies, disability is not to be thought of as an overwhelming illness or injury to the body (the medical model) or as a limitation resulting merely from social consensus and barriers (the social model), but to be reconceptualised and interpreted as a contingent, socio-cultural or socio-historical construct (the cultural model). We therefore have also to ask, for example, how far literary models of depiction are involved in the creation and consolidation of scientific, cultural and social ideas of difference in a society and so of a narrative construction of disability as a negative distinguishing characteristic, for example by means of binary oppositions such as normal-deviant, disabled-not disabled or affected-not affected. Are people with a disability represented in their individuality and with their various talents as part of human diversity, or (un)consciously reduced to a few stigmatising distinguishing features and turned into images contrasting with an allegedly desirable normality? Do literary texts contribute to enabling people with a disability to take part in all aspects of life, to be seen and heard in the community and in education, or do they tend to be counter-productive, by resurrecting and recycling clichés from cultural memory? From a dis/ability-critical perspective – especially in view of the formative influence of the bible on culture over centuries – even New Testament healing stories must therefore be read with a view to seeing whether they contribute or have contributed to the construct of disability, or instead through their inclusive images of hope promote the that all people may participate in all areas of life both in the present and the future.

II Normalising Assumptions – a perspective from medical anthropology

Even on a first level of interpretation from the perspective of medical anthropology, the healing story in Mk 7.31-37 looks ambivalent when contrasted with a dis/ability-critical hermeneutics. From a religious studies perspective, and in view of the healing materials and techniques described, the narrative unit shows parallels with a Hellenistic miracle story,[5] though it does not seek to show Jesus simply as an all-powerful doctor, but as someone particularly concerned with to people in distress. On the other hand, if we apply modern criteria for a successful participatory and communicative relationship, the exchange and encounter between the two main figures involved are rather one-sided. Unnamed helpers bring a deaf, stammering man, who also remains anonymous, to Jesus with the request that he should lay his hand on him (v. 32), probably as a gesture of healing transmitting power. As a way of keeping the treatment that follows secret, Jesus takes the deaf man to one side, puts his fingers into his ears and touches his tongue (v. 33). Then Jesus looks up to heaven and sighs, both signs that again indicate drawing on super-human power, and says to the deaf man, 'Ephphatha!' (v. 34), which as a word from a foreign language is meant to remain unintelligible and act as a magic word. The translation ('Be opened!'), is intended for the readers of the gospel.

The text does not allow for any real medical diagnosis, but there is a clear expectation that the deaf man who can barely speak is healed and enters majority society with the normally required communication abilities. A striking feature is the contrast between the passivity of the deaf man – as readers we learn nothing of any gesture of agreement or refusal – and the activity of the people who bring him to Jesus; from today's perspective, at least, appears to be an action involving little communication and expressing well-meant, but ultimately paternalistic solidarity. Even when in v.35 it is emphasised that the deaf man's ears are immediately opened and his tongue is released, this is a confirmation of his healing and of Jesus' healing power, but does not allow the healed man to say anything, and bring him out of his role as a mere, anonymous visual aid. In contrast, Jesus, as previously mentioned, is certainly not portrayed merely as a Hellenistic miracle-worker, whose successful healing skill is the point of the story, but as very human: he develops a personal relationship to the deaf man through his gestures and physical touching. Whether Jesus restores him to his community after he has taken him aside, remains unclear, however. What today appears as not very inclusive may also be explained by the very emphatic command at the end of the healing that it should be kept secret (v. 36), which has the function of preventing Jesus from being understood precisely not as an unusual wonder-worker – as it were, in competition with the Hellenistic miraculous healers, but of interpreting his miracles in the light of his cross and resurrection as an expression of the dawning of the kingdom of God. Nevertheless in vv 36-37 it becomes clear that the command to silence has precisely the opposite effect: the more Jesus tells them not to, the more they 'proclaim' it and are 'astounded beyond measure'. The healed man, in contrast, is not mentioned, not even, as might be expected, to hear that he praises God. In dis/ability-critical terms, even after his healing, as at the beginning of the story, his role remains a silent, non-speaking one, designed primarily to contribute to the story that confirms Jesus' power.

III. Capacities to recognise – a spiritual and Christological perspective

On closer examination of the context, the interpretation of the healing story in Mk 7.31-37 moves from an understanding interested in medical facts and inter-personal relations to a spiritual and Christological interpretation that starts from a metaphorical meaning of hearing or not hearing in the sense of an ability to recognise or a process of understanding of who Jesus in fact is (Mk 4.41) that has not advanced sufficiently – either among the disciples or among the readers. This theme is announced several times early on in Jesus' discourse on the parables (Mk 4.1-34), for example with the appeal at the beginning of the parable of the Sower (Mk 4.3) and the concluding call to be attentive: 'Let anyone with ears to hear listen!' (Mk 4.9). The issue here is not just about hearing sounds, but primarily about hearing with understanding and taking the message to heart. The disciples are again and again shown as lacking in the necessary insight (Mk 6.52). Even after the healing of the deaf man and the two multiplications of loaves (Mk 6.30-44; 8.1-10), their lack of understanding is once more clear: instead of wondering about the yeast of the Pharisees and the yeast of Herod (Mk 8.15), they only worry about having enough to eat because they have only brought one loaf for the crossing of the lake Mk 8.14, 16). Jesus rebukes them yet again: 'Do you still not perceive or understand? Are your hearts hardened? Do you have eyes, and fail to see? Do you have ears, and fail to hear? And do you not remember?' (Mk 8.17c-18; v. 18 includes a quotation from Is 5.21). They can answer his question about the number of baskets of fragments left over after each of the two feeding miracles (Mk 8.19-20), but Jesus still reacts with the same reproachful question (8.21b): 'Do you not yet understand?' What conclusions the disciples are meant to draw from the collected scraps of bread Jesus or the evangelist leaves open, though the twice repeated 'not yet' (8.17, 21) allows for the hope that the disciples will soon get insight and come to faith in him. The following story about the healing of a blind man (Mk 8.22-26), just like its twin story about the healing of the deaf man with a hearing impediment in Mk 7.31-37, becomes symbolic evidence for eventual slow growth of trusting faith; this reaches a climax in the story of the healing of the blind Bartimaeus (Mk 10.46-52), which ends with the cured man immediately becoming a disciple. In this way all three healing stories metaphorically reflect the hope of progress in understanding and discipleship on the part of the disciples, and on the part of the readers too.

In addition, the fact that the healing of the deaf man takes place in the Decapolis (Mk 7.31) underlines the fact that Jesus' proclamation with powerful actions that God's rule has begun (Mk 1.14-15) is also intended for the Gentiles (cf also the miracle stories in Mk 7.24-30 and 8.1-10), and that, as it were, he is also opening their ears.

While the possibility of growth in the capacity for recognition is important as Mark's gospel continues, from a dis/ability-critical perspective this approach creates a considerable problem in the context of the gospel, because deafness and blindness are treated as metaphors for religious learning difficulties and so in the end deaf and blind people become images or figures to which negative associations are attached. If cures for deafness and blindness, and other Markan healing stories, are the expression of a prior need for trusting faith (see e.g. Mk 2.5; 5.34; 9.23-24) and metaphorical examples of the overcoming of inadequate insight into the significance of Jesus, deaf and blind people who are not healed inevitably become symbols of inadequate understanding or lack of faith.

Illustrated by Mk 7.31-37

IV Visions of perfection – an eschatological and soteriological perspective

If the healing of a deaf man who can barely speak (Mk 7.31-19) can in its context be interpreted as a metaphor for the hope that both the faith of the disciples and that of the readers will grow, Jesus' later reproachful question to the disciples asking whether they did not yet understand (Mk 8.21) is, as we saw, all the more puzzling since they have in fact correctly answered his question about how many baskets of scraps were left over after each of the two mass feedings (Mk 6.30-44; 8.1-10). The key feature of both feeding miracles is probably not just that 5,000 and 4,000 were able to be well fed with a few loaves and fishes (Mk 6.38, 44). Rather the twelve baskets full of scraps of bread and fish (Mk 6.43) or the seven baskets of bread scraps (Mk 8.8) point to an abundance that goes beyond the present moment. This theme of abundance points to an abundant feast for the last days and so creates an image of hope that again draws on the original paradisical state. By interweaving periods in this way, the multiplications of loaves not only change the world they narrate, but can also begin to become reality in the present of the readers by feeding protest against social injustices and hope for a better future.[6]

A comparable perspective of hope for future wholeness with a reference back to God's good creation can be found immediately before the feeding of the four thousand (Mk 8.1-10), when the author of Mark has the crowd express amazement after the healing of the deaf man and say: 'He has done everything well; he even makes the deaf to hear and the dumb to speak.' (Mk 7.37). With the play on two Old Testament texts, Gen. 1.31 ('God saw everything that he had made, and indeed, it was very good.') and Is 35.5-6 ('Then the eyes of the blind shall be opened, and the ears of the deaf unstopped; then the lame shall leap like a deer, and the tongue of the speechless sing for joy. For waters shall break forth in the wilderness, and streams in the desert.') the evangelist emphasises forcefully that 'God himself is at work as creator bringing eschatological wholeness,'[7] and food in abundance and the healing of the sick are to be understood as signs that the end-time is dawning.[8] If the interweaving of historical periods evoked in the case of the two feeding miracles is also transferred to the healing of the deaf man – or to other healing stories – this means, by analogy, that the change that takes place in the time of the story, that is, the healing, must be derived from an ideal of the body to be expected at the end-time, which in turn corresponds to the original state in Paradise. So, just as the abundance in the story cannot relieve hunger here and now, but allows the present to be seen as surmountable in view of the future, the power of Jesus described in the story can act in the here and now of the readers and make illness and disability appear in the end, in the light of the bodily perfection we may expect, merely transitory. If in this approach to interpretation feeding miracles are to be understood as stories of hope and protest, then healing miracles too are to be interpreted as hope that illness and suffering can be overcome, and as a protest against them. From such a perspective, biblical healing narratives stress the conviction, completely in accord with a medical model of disability, that everything must be done to make it possible to 'heal' disability here and now in the present, or at least to 'relieve' it.

V Exclusive offers versus an inclusive dis/ability critical perspective

By cutting through everyday experience in this way and transcending expectations modelled on a sense of reality, healing narratives unlock at the level of narrative – especially with their allusions to prophetic visions of wholeness – 'exclusive offers' and 'wonderful possibilities' for readers today as well as those of the evangelist's time. But from an inclusive or dis/ability-critical view, as noted in the introduction, these images of hope and the unthinking identification of healing and wholeness also implicitly transport images of what is generally seen as normal and desirable. If Jesus' healings are a sign of liberation and a new start, illness and disability in contrast point to a state that must be overcome. As the following example of interpretation shows, biblical healing stories can very quickly appear exclusive, because they do not provide hope, either for a person here and now or for the future, that all people, independently of their physical, mental or intellectual situation, can participate. This pointed reflection is by Sabine Fries, herself deaf and now professor of sign language interpretation, and was written in 1997, when she was in her first job as chaplain to deaf people:

'An incredible miracle?' Well, unfortunately for me this story has a sting in the tail. That deaf and dumb man in Mark's gospel can hear again.

Illustrated by Mk 7.31-37

We can't! Being able to hear, a miracle? The wholeness we all hope for? Really I can't imagine it at all. I am as I am, that is, as God created me. And I also believe that God wants this life as a deaf person to be my life. And that means that everything that comes with deafness is part of me. Everything, sign language, the deaf community, the hassles of everyday life in a hearing world that I come up against day after day. And even when I often get angry that I can't hear properly and miss a whole lot, and even when I see the difficulties other deaf people have to struggle with, I notice that the miracle of the healing of the deaf and dumb man doesn't really say anything to me. It provokes too much resistance in me, makes me think of the gods of medicine, of ear operations and technical gimmicks. No, I don't want that sort of miracle from my creator God... I would like to keep my identity, my equilibrium, my imagination. I've come to feel at home on the planet of the deaf community. That is why the gospel of the healing of the deaf and dumb man has always felt a bit alien to me, a bit like imagining a journey to another planet. Healing and miracles leave me cold, and really what I would like for us today is a different application of the text.[9]

This is only one example, and not every deaf person in Germany or across the world – something like 0.01 % of the overall population - will see things in the same way – that's also an effect of human diversity. But on the other hand, it's all the more problematic if people who can hear become the only standard for normality or for the supposedly correct interpretation of biblical healing narratives. Every reader should let themselves be disturbed, so to say, by another person's reading and let themselves be challenged, as for example when the chaplain to people with hearing problems in the diocese of Limburg, Christian Enke, puts forward a diametrically opposite image of hope in a current article:

> In heaven can all the deaf hear? That is what we might think when we read *The healing of the deaf and dumb man* in the Gospel (Mk 7.35) and Isaiah's Advent prophecies of leaping deer and dumb people singing (Is 35.6). I also suspect that in the eulogies at many funerals we may hear disturbing and macabre words like: 'Now at last he or she can hear (or see or walk...) properly.'... I imagine that all that matters is: there everyone is really well. But ideally we ought to be able to experience

this in the community here on earth as a foretaste of God's kingdom, in which everyone gets along splendidly... and that doesn't mean everyone has to speak Latin, but perhaps everyone can do sign language.'[10]

If we try to take account of both the context of the healing narratives and that of today's readers, clearly the hope based on the world-changing power of Jesus' miracles and the awareness of the changes wrought by human fragility on interpretation do not coincide. A tension of this sort disturbs our reading and leads to contradictory interpretations, but only at first sight. These interpretations can also be seen as complementary and as the expression of an art of interpretation that precisely in this way reflects the diversity and fragility of human beings. Rethinking in the face of human fragility – even in the field of biblical healing narratives – leads as a consequence to images of hope that have the power to overturn the boundaries of customary concepts of normality and other categories. With Susanne Krahe, a theologian and writer who became blind after completing her studies, we can, for example, imagine a creation 'in which "becoming whole" only surpasses the broken present to the extent that the non-whole, the bent and less able is no longer regarded as disturbing,' and in which it is part of humanity 'to welcome the disabled, in their disability, as a part of creation's diversity, instead of complaining about them as sub-standard.'[11]

Translated by Francis McDonagh

Notes

1. The description 'healing of a deaf and dumb man' is deliberately avoided in this article because it resembles the term 'deaf mute', which as the German Association of hearing Loss Sufferers (https://www.gehoerlosen-bund.de/faq/geh%C3%B6rlosigkeit [22 March 2020]) writes, 'is outdated and felt by many sufferers from hearing loss to be pejorative and discriminatory. People suffering from hearing loss are deaf but by no means dumb, as they are able to express themselves in sign language and also to speak. Accordingly the terms "hearing loss sufferer" or "deaf" are used. The term "deaf" (without "mute") is increasingly popular as it corresponds to the English word "deaf" and, unlike "hearing loss sufferer" has no negative connotation.'
2. Julia Watts Belser and Marie Hecke, ,'"Die Augen der Blinden werden sehen" Jes 29,18, *Predigthilfe & Materialien für die Gemeinde zum 27.01.2018*, Berlin, pp 25–35, 26–28.
3. For a detailed account, see Markus Schiefer Ferrari, *Exklusive Angebote: Biblische Heilungsgeschichten inklusiv gelesen*, Ostfildern, 2017.

Illustrated by Mk 7.31-37

4. See Markus Schiefer Ferrari, 'Dis/ability Studies,' *Das Wissenschaftlich-Religionspädagogische Lexikon im Internet (WiReLex)*, 2019, at https://www.bibelwissenschaft.de/stichwort/200578/ (consulted 28 September 2020).
5. For this section, see, for example, Nadine Ueberschaer, 'Mit allen Sinnen Leben! (Die Heilung eines Taubstummen) Mk 7,31–37', in Ruben Zimmermann (ed.), *Kompendium der frühchristlichen Wundererzählungen: Volume 1: Die Wunder Jesu*, Gütersloh, 2013, pp 323–331; Detlev Dormeyer, 'Die Wunder im Markusevangelium. Hinführung', in Zimmermann, Kompendium der frühchristlichen Wundererzählungen, pp 193–202; Reinhard von Bendemann, 'Auditus et testamentum – Die Heilung des Tauben/Stummen in der Dekapolis (Mk 7,31–37)', in Wilfried Härle et al. (ed.), *Systematisch Praktisch: Festschrift Reiner Preul* (MThSt 80), Marburg, 2005, pp 55 69.
6. See Michael Labahn, 'Wunder verändern die Welt. Überlegungen zum sinnkonstituierenden Charakter von Wundererzählungen am Beispiel der so- genannten "Geschenkwunder"', in Bernd Kollmann and Ruben Zimmermann (ed.), *Hermeneutik der frühchristlichen Wundererzählungen: Geschichtliche, literarische und rezeptionsorientierte Perspektiven* (WUNT 339), Tübingen, 2014, pp 369–393.
7. Ludger Schenke, *Das Markusevangelium: Literarische Eigenart – Text und Kommentierung*, Stuttgart, 2005, p. 191.
8. See also on the next section Markus Schiefer Ferrari, 'Blindenheilung für Blinde. Wechselnde Perspektiven auf Mk 8,22–26', *I&M. Zeitschrift für den katholischen Religionsunterricht* 1 (2019), 24–31.
9. Sabine Fries, Evening Prayer for the 2nd German Cultural Festival of Deaf People in the Annenkirche, Dresden, on Saturday 25 October 1997 (held in German Sign Language): https://archiv.taubenschlag.de/cms_pics/sabine_fries.pdf (Accessed 29.09.20).
10. Christian Enke, 'Vielleicht können ja alle gebärden', *Feinschwarz.net – Theologisches Feuilleton*, 28 February 2020, at: https://www.feinschwarz.net/vielleicht-koennen-ja-alle-gebaerden/ (accessed 29.09.20).
11. Susanne Krahe and Ulrike Metternich, Ulrike, 'Kraft oder Kränkung – Heilungsgeschichten im Neuen Testament kontrovers diskutiert', in Ilse Falk et al. (ed.), *So ist mein Leib. Alter, Krankheit und Behinderung – feministisch-theologische Anstöße, hg. im Auftrag der Evangelischen Frauen in Deutschland (EFiD)*, Gütersloh, 2012, pp 25–43, 38.

Approaching Disability: Pastoral History and Practice Analyzed Through the Models of the Church

LUCA BADETTI

How have people with disabilities been part of the pastoral life of the Church throughout history? This undoubtedly is a broad and multi-layered question that demands critical analysis across its complex facets. First of all, the very notion of disability is to be problematized. Moving beyond disability, the very notion of a history of the "life of the Church" might sound like an all-encompassing exhaustive statement that actually is only part of a much wider and shifting story. The article works with these critical understandings and questions and analyse the Church's pastoral approach – both theoretical and practical – towards disability. To avoid writing a totalizing historical narrative that overly simplifies history and trumps upon all the unrecognized and silent "little histories", the option is not for a chronological presentation of Church disability history. The article explores the Church's understanding and action as it pertains to disability making use of Avery Dulles' six models of the Church. And does not seek to give an exhaustive historical account, but rather seeks to present historical moments, themes, persons and practices pertinent to the theme so as to elicit both some understanding of the past but also encourage critical questions moving forward.

I Introduction

How have people with disabilities been part of the pastoral life of the

Approaching Disability

Church throughout history? This undoubtedly is a broad and multi-layered question that demands critical analysis across its complex facets.

First of all, the very notion of disability is to be problematized. Who is identified as "people with disabilities"? Disability is a fairly modern concept. How to apply this to a past that did not have current disability "criteria"? Is disability an individual reality or a social construct, or a mix of the two? In addition, not all people with impairments identify as being disabled – even if they are classified as such by some external standard. Should they be included in such a survey?

Moving beyond disability, the very notion of a history of the "life of the Church" might sound like an all-encompassing exhaustive statement that actually is only part of a much wider and shifting story. Disability history in general has often been recorded by people without disabilities, which is problematic. People with disabilities have been spoken about and written about, but their agency in telling their own stories and understandings of the Church has too seldom been given space.

It is with these critical understandings and questions that I write this analysis of the Church's pastoral approach – both theoretical and practical – towards disability.

To avoid writing a totalizing historical narrative that overly simplifies history and trumps upon all the unrecognized and silent "little histories", I have decided not to opt for a chronological presentation of Church disability history. I have decided, instead, to explore the Church's understanding and action as it pertains to disability making use of Avery Dulles' six models of the Church...[1] For the previously mentioned reasons, this article does not seek to give an exhaustive historical account, but rather seeks to present historical moments, themes, persons and practices pertinent to the theme so as to elicit both some understanding of the past but also encourage critical questions moving forward

II Overview of disability construction and identity through time

Not only may the Church be interpreted through different models, but also disability. To better understand how disability will be approached throughout this article, we will make use, once again, of models. Not Dulles' models, but the models of disability that the discipline of Disability Studies has helped popularize.

A very common model through which disability has traditionally been approached is the medical model: this model views disability as a condition present in the person - an individual reality "to be fixed." The social model, a term coined by Mike Oliver, switched the focus.[2] Grounded in the UK disability rights movement, it emphasized disability as an oppressive social construct created by those barriers, attitudes and social structures that disable people with impairments. Notice the difference between impairments, which can be physical in nature and requiring medical attention/supports, and disability, as that which society creates.

Besides these two major models, other models have been used to contextualize disability. The minority model, for example, emphasizes the political and cultural struggle of people with disabilities who have faced oppression through time. The identity model frames disability as a personal and group identity marker. The limits model of disability, developed by theologian Deborah B. Creamer, underlines how having limits is part of humanity.[3]

This article won't interpret disability only according to one model, but will do so bringing into play different approaches, also considering that the term disability has seen various developments through time. Before the nineteenth century, being disabled implied being disadvantaged by laws that prevented participation in civic and economic life, while later on, onto the twentieth century, the emphasis was put on biological functioning.[4] The idea of "normalcy" itself, against which disability is often defined, expanded when, with the development of statistics, human traits' statistical average began to be equated with the norm.[5]

The Church has often approached disability as an individual condition in need of care and support, a servant Church that has sought to show genuine concern and attentiveness towards persons with disabilities but that has also tended to treat them as passive subjects on the receiving end of the pastoral action: pastoral decisions have too often been made "for" people with disabilities and not by the them. This, however, has not always been the case. The Church has grown in many ways not only in affirming the agency of the disabled person, but also in making space for people with disabilities to be agents of the pastoral action themselves. This may be seen not only in the removal of pastoral, community and structural barriers that prevent their full participation in the life of the church, but also in the inclusion of their voices and experiences in the development of Christian community life, a community of disciples that is enriched by a shared humanity manifest in the uniqueness of each person.

III The servant Church and disability: Caring for disability

Out of the different Church models, the one that might most often be associated with disability is the one connected to service and practical care. The Christian community has recurrently approached people with disabilities as people to be cared for.

The idea of Christian service is deeply connected to that of charity, a loving selfless response towards the other. Christian service is therefore not simply an action, a "doing things for," but also an action that is done with a loving spirit, with care. It is not surprising that, although in ancient Greece and ancient Rome the practice of infanticide was at times used to eliminate those who were considered to have defects, Judeo-Christian values renounced this practice.[6] The early Christian church's stance of welcome and care towards those that many would have otherwise rejected helped change the course of history. In medieval times, a period during which the Church often sponsored almshouses, parishes provided an early form of welfare.[7] Today, across the world many disability ministries in dioceses and religious communities (for example, the communities inspired by the spirituality and the work of Fr. Luigi Guanella[8]) protect, care for and speak on behalf of persons with disabilities.

As important as care and service are, the idea of service, however, can sometimes present challenges too, or a shadow side. In its pastoral service approach, the Church has often approached the disabled person as the one that is poor, suffering and needy, and the non-disabled person as the one who has the power to give, care and serve. In other words, there can be a shadow side to the idea of "service to the disabled," namely that of creating a unilateral approach in which the non-disabled person holds the power and the disabled person is the passive recipient of it.

To give an idea of this, let's take an art-work that gives us an image of urban society around 1500 and that was commissioned by the regents of the Holy Spirit Almshouse in Alkmaar, namely *The Seven Works of Mercy*, a 1504 seven-panels polyptych painting by Master of Alkmaar that depicts the corporal works of mercy of Catholic tradition.[9] It is particularly telling here to pinpoint Hughes analysis of it.[10] People with disabilities are portrayed by the artist even if the work of mercy does not directly relate to disability. In the "Feeding the Hungry" panel, for example, there is a sitting non-ambulant beggar and a blind man waiting for bread from two givers (a blind person seems also to be portrayed in *Welcoming Strangers*), and in *Living Drink to the Thirsty* a wealthy man gives sustenance to a man who has a walking impairment. People with disabilities are included in the artwork, even if the primary narrative or, to borrow a concept popularized by Adichie,[11] the "single story" being told about people with disabilities, seems to be that disability equals being needy – and being cared for as a result. Hughes notes how this polyptych, created during the transition between Middles Ages and Early Modernity, did not focus so much on the spiritual wealth of those with disabilities, but on people with disabilities as instruments for non-disabled people's spiritual capital.

In recent times, Masters wrote of David Perry, a father of a boy with Down Syndrome, who expressed concern about Pope Francis' representation of people with disabilities in *Amoris Laetitia*, as well as on Twitter, where a post mentioned how *people with disabilities are a gift for the family and an opportunity to grow in love, mutual aid and unit.*[12] Perry warns against objectifying and infantilizing the person with a disability.[13] Masters writes how, *There are some real concerns with seeing someone as a vehicle for me to do good.*[14]

The spirit of service and care has given rise to wonderful acts of care and support towards people with disabilities. At times, however, it has also become too one sided. It is time to bring greater attention to those stories of people with disabilities that provide care and support to others! In the *As I am* video documentary, *Take Care of You*, for example, Raffaella Monterosso, a woman with Down Syndrome living in an Italian L'Arche community, accompanies her elderly father on a wheelchair,[15] shifting notions of disability service. Stories and images like these can help reframe disability narratives, even across the ideas of service and care.

IV The sacramental and institutional Church: Representing and addressing disability

Throughout the history of the Church, there are various examples of Christian individuals that may today be classified as being disabled. Third

Approaching Disability

Order Dominican Margaret of Castello, for example, was born blind with a curvature of the spine that made walking difficult. Margaret was rejected by her family.[16] She was abandoned in a church and the poor of the town helped take care of her. Although the town's poor formed community around her, in Margaret's story the attention/care she received was not unilateral. In fact, she eventually started a school for children. Hers is not only a story of care received, but also of care given.

German Benedictine abbess Hildegard of Bingen appears to have lived with an invisible disability, as someone with chronic illness going through migraine attacks.[17] She is not so much remembered for this, however, but is rather remembered as a prominent female spirituality figure, a pharmacist and musician. Although often people with disabilities are portrayed as inspirational just because of disability, Hildegard is a sign that disability need not be the primary identifier or the all-encompassing identity marker of a person. Even if disability is part of a person's experience, it is not the only element that characterizes a person.

If the examples of these witnesses symbolize grace shining through impairment, it must be noted that too often, in the Church, disability has been treated as an inferior reality through ecclesial and institutional ableist practices, for example in regards to people with disabilities' access to the sacraments. Within Christian anthropology, there have been various emphases in regards to what it means for human beings to be made in the image of God, some focusing on intellectual capacity and others centred more around the heart. Suffice to say here that the emphasis on the former may be connected to how, in the pastoral realm, people with intellectual disabilities have been denied access to the sacrament of the Eucharist (and other sacraments as well) because of a perceived lack of the (intellectual) capacity to assent to the reception of the Body and Blood of Christ. However, as Maliszewska points out, „all people are known to be equal before God. There can hardly be any doubt regarding the fact that intellectual excellence or high IQ level are not necessarily bound with faith."".[18]

Surely, more modern developments have shown a move away from an overly ratio-centric understanding of sacramental assent. For example, the United States Conference of Catholic Bishops' Guidelines for the Celebration of the Sacraments with Persons with Disabilities provide a pastoral note pointing that „the criterion for reception of Holy Communion is the same for persons with intellectual and developmental disabilities as for all persons, namely, that the person be able to "distinguish the body of Christ from ordinary food", "even if this recognition is evidenced through manner, gesture, or reverential silence rather than verbally".[19] In so doing, however, it pinpoints to the 913 Code of Canon Law section that deals with the administration of the Holy Eucharist to children.[20] The cultural infantilization of people with intellectual disabilities is a problem that has not ceased to happen, and Church practices and regulations need to ensure that they avoid any association that can easily lead to infantilizing adults with disabilities, which can also impact access to other sacrament, including that of Matrimony and Holy Orders.

V The Church as herald: Announcing disability

Christian interpretations of disability have generally included seeing disability as a punishment for sin, as a test of faith, as inspiration or as a mystery.[21] How disability has been talked through time, also within the Church, has been influenced by these understandings. Undoubtedly, Scripture has been a strong basis for disability interpretations to this day. Suffice to say that there are different images that are associated with disability and that can give rise to a variety of different interpretations. The Church has often treated disability in such vein. In 2016, for example, the Jubilee for the Sick and Persons with Disabilities grouped together sickness and disability, which is pastorally problematic. Does this run the danger of equating the pastoral approach towards those who are ill to those who have disabilities? During his homily pope Francis spoke of the Jubilee being devoted not only to the sick but also to the „bearers of disabilities" (par. 1).[22] Years earlier, John Paul II mentioned how, "In your bodies and in your lives, dear brothers and sisters, you express an intense hope of redemption (...) every person marked by a physical or mental difficulty lives a sort of existential *advent*, waiting for a *redemption* that will be fully manifest, for him as for everyone, only at the end of time".[23] Disability, in both Francis' and John Paul II's approaches, appears to imply an individual, physical and suffering dimension. It is important not to forget the wider socio-cultural forces that disable people with impairments, and that people with disabilities can be happy with their minds and bodies (and even proud of being disabled), while also suffering because of isolation and prejudice, which pastoral action needs to address.

Moving alongside the greater emphasis on disability self-determination and empowerment, the Committee for the Jubilee Day of the Community with Persons with Disabilities addressed how persons with disabilities are, just like anyone, directly responsible for their lives and stories; not only is the Gospel message destined for them, but they themselves announce it.[24] This is a key difference between a pastoral theology that sees persons with disabilities as passive recipients of the Gospel message and the Church's action to one that views them as heralds, as active agents of announcing the Gospel.

VI The Church as community of disciplines: An inclusive journey of belonging

The idea of community is central to the identity of the church and at the heart of its pastoral action. The disciples were called on a growth journey of conversion together. Community needs to be inclusive, and allow that to be a graced occasion for growth in communion across human differences. It is good news that the Church's pastoral life has grown in its inclusion of persons with disabilities in a way that fosters their sense of belonging and affirms their presence and gifts. The example of L'Arche faith communities pinpoints to this. In L'Arche homes and workshops across the world, in fact, people with and without intellectual disabilities share life and a common mission, which includes making known the gifts of persons with intellectual disabilities, revealed through relationships that are mutually transformative, and engaging in diverse cultures, working together towards a society that is more human.[25] Similarly, Faith and Light communities seek to create bonds of friendship between persons with and without disabilities, bringing together persons with disabilities, family members and friends.[26]

Many other realities that actively promote community inclusion of persons with disabilities exist. The work of the Community of Sant'Egidio is one of them, as shown, for instance, in its Roman Trattoria degli Amici (*Friends Restaurant*), which employs people with disabilities and welcomes volunteers, and its art exhibits showcasing works of disabled artists.[27] At the level of parishes, great steps have been made - from making structures, liturgy participation and ways of worship more accessible, to ensuring people with disabilities take part in meaningful roles of church presence and participation.[28] This may remind us of the theological vision of the church as the body of Christ, in which each member has a uniquely important role (1 Cor. 12). Even in more recent times, however, greater inclusion and accessibility remains a need. In 2016, The Kairos Forum and the Pontifical Council for Culture called together, for a Living Fully conference, persons with disabilities, disability theology scholars and faith communities representatives to learn from each other. The charter that was created on the occasion called for a way forward in living an ordinary culture of belonging for all.[29]

It is hoped that inclusion and belonging will grow ever more in the pastoral action of the Church, as they are part of its very identity and mission. Within this, it is hoped that persons with disabilities will be empowered and supported (as needed) to be the pastoral agents that will write the next pages of pastoral disability history themselves.

Notes

1. Dulles, Avery, *Models of the Church*. New York: Image, 2002.
2. Oliver, Mike, *Social Work with Disabled People*. Basingtoke, UK: Macmillan, 1983.
3. Creamer, Deborah B., *Disability and Christian theology: Embodied Limits and Constructive Possibilities*. Oxford: Oxford University Press, 2009.
4. Francis, Leslie and Silvers, Anita, Perspectives on the meaning of "disability". *AMA Journal of Ethics*, *18*(10), 1025-1033.
5. Davis, Lennard J., 'Constructing normalcy. The bell curve, the novel, and the invention of the disabled body in the nineteenth century'. In Lennard J. Davis (Ed.), *The Disability Studies Reader* (2nd ed.), New York, NY: Routledge, 2006, 3-16.
6. Gualtieri, Camimmo T., Brain injury and mental retardation: Psychopharmacology and neuropsychiatry. Philadelphia: Lippincott Williams & Wilkins Publishers, 2002.
7. Hughes, Bill, *A Historical Sociology of Disability: Human Validity and Invalidity from Antiquity to Early Modernity*. (1 ed.) (Routledge Advances in Disability Studies). London, UK: Taylor & Francis Ltd. 2019.
8. See Servants of Charity, Guanellian Formation. Retrieved from https://servantsofcharity.org/guanellian-formation; The Communities of Don Guanella and Divine Providence (n.d.) *What we do*. Retrieved from https://dgdpcommunities.org/what-we-do-2/.
9. Europeana, *The Seven Works of Mercy*. Retrieved from https://www.europeana.eu/en/item/90402/SK_A_2815.
10. Hughes, *A Historical Sociology of Disability*.
11. Adichie Chimamanda N., *The danger of a single story* | Chimamanda Ngozi Adichie. Retrieved from https://www.ted.com/talks/chimamanda_ngozi_adichie_the_danger_of_a_single_story?language=en

12. Francis (2016, April 9). Tweet-People with disabilities are a gift. Retrieved from https://twitter.com/pontifex/status/718710082406473728
13. Perry, D. (2016). *'Amoris Laetitia' reflects narrow view of disabled persons*. Retrieved from http://www.cruxnow.com/church/2016/04/12/amoris-laetitia-reflects-narrow-view-of-disabled-persons/
14. Masters, Anne, An opportunity for charity? A Catholic tradition in understanding disability and its impact on ministry. *Journal of Disability & Religion*, *20*(3), 218-227, here 223; cfr. Francis, Amoris Laetitia (the joy of love): On love in the family. Cincinnati, OH: Beacon Publishing, par. 47; Id., Tweet-People with disabilities are a gift. Retrieved from https://twitter.com/pontifex/status/718710082406473728; Perry, David M., *'Amoris Laetitia' reflects narrow view of disabled persons*. Retrieved from http://www.cruxnow.com/church/2016/04/12/amoris-laetitia-reflects-narrow-view-of-disabled-persons/.
15. L'Arche Internationale. (2016, March 17). #AsIAm Documentary | Raffaella's Story | Take Care of You | Episode 4. Retrieved from https://www.youtube.com/watch?v=tD_DFwlDbXw.
16. Yong, Amos, Theology and Down Syndrome. Waco: Baylor University Press 2007.
17. Maddocks, Fiona, *Hildegard of Bingen: The Woman of Her Age*. New York: Doubleday, 2001; Sacks Oliver, Migraine: understanding a common disorder. Berkeley: University of California Press, 1985.
18. Maliszewska, Anna, *The invisible Church: People with profound intellectual disabilities and the Eucharist – A Catholic perspective*. Journal of Disability & Religion, 23(2), 197–210, here 202.
19. United States Conference of Catholic Bishops, Guidelines for the Celebration of the Sacraments with Persons with Disabilities. Retrieved from: www.usccb.org/about/divine-worship/policies/guidelines-sacraments-persons-with-disabilities.cfm, #22.
20. See Code of Canon Law, c. 913, §2, c. 914 [1983]).
21. Creamer, *Disability and Christian theology.*
22. Francis, Extraordinary Jubilee of Mercy. Jubilee for the Sick and Persons with Disabilities. Homily of His Holiness Pope Francis. Retrieved from http://www.vatican.va/content/francesco/en/homilies/2016/documents/papa-francesco_20160612_omelia-giubileo-ammalati-disabili.html
23. John Paul II (December 3). Jubilee of the Disabled. Homily of John Paul II. Retrieved from https://w2.vatican.va/content/john-paul-ii/en/homilies/2000/documents/hf_jp-ii_hom_20001203_jubildisabled.html, sect. 2.
24. Comitato per la Giornata Giubilare della Comunità con le Persone con Disabilità, Scheda di Preparazione alla Giornata Giubilare del 3 Dicembre 2000. Terza scheda. La Persona con Disabilità: Soggetto - Protagonista di Pastorale. Retrieved from http://www.vatican.va/jubilee_2000/jubilevents/jub_disabled_20001203_scheda3_it.htm
25. L'Arche International, Identity and Mission. Retrieved from https://www.larche.org/identity-and-mission.
26. Faith and Light, In the society and the Church. Retrieved from https://www.faithandlight.org/rubriques/haut/our-mission/in-the-community
27. Zenit Staff (November 15). Friends Tap Talents of the Disabled. Retrieved from: https://zenit.org/articles/friends-tap-talents-of-the-disabled/
28. See also United States Conference of Catholic Bishops, Welcome and Justice for Persons with Disabilities. Washington, DC: USCCB Publishing, 1998.
29. Statement from Living Fully 2016 - Disability, Culture and Faith: A Celebration, Cultura e Fede, 24(3), 208-219.

Rebuilding Christian Mission from the Perspective of 'Discriminated Differently Abled'

HUANG, PO HO

The disputes about the usage of the terminology between "disability" and "differently abled" caused in ecumenical church communities reflected different yet important concerns of the issue and its theological reflections, as well the nature and position of Christian mission. The concept of disability has to do with accessibility of participation. While social construction has not only construct the identity of a group of people but also construct an environment to prevent them to participate. The issue thus involves a critical matter of "power", an exclusive power that majority people exercised to preclude heterogeneous individuals. This dominant superior power of exclusion hence needs to be examined and dealt with theologically.

I Introduction
Despite of the obvious discrimination and exclusive position expressed in their Bible, Christian Churches has been considered as one of the most attentive organizations toward the so called "disabled people". According to Samuel Kabue: "The term 'disability' is a creation of the modern society in its attempt to group people with different characteristics perceived to have related or similar effects on the human life."[1] He points out that, it is not a term that existed either in the Western or the African traditions. The Judeo-Christian tradition too did not have this type of classification as it described individuals in accordance to their specific infirmities. This explains why the term will not be found in the Bible.[2] The definition of

the term can be traced to two interests of models, namely medical model and social construction. The medical model is supported largely by the caregivers, health workers and academics, while social construction is embraced mostly by the people with disabilities through their movements.[3]

In fact, the so call "disability" can be distinguished by the cases of innate and those postnatal. The postnatal cases are acquired by various reasons: genetic inheritance, illness, accidents and senescence. In certain degree we can say all human being are potentially, sooner or later, for perennial or short duration to experience "disabled". This means that the so-called "disability" is a different nature of the same phenomenon. Some cases of the impairment are curable and some are not. This explains the significance of the arguments of the two models of medical and sociological aspects.

II Disabled and power manipulation

The terminologies used to describe these human physical infirmities are diverse; descriptions such as "handicaps", "disabled" or "people with disability" are prevailing in modern society, but there was a period of time when "differently abled" has been used to reflect inclusiveness by the ecumenical communities. However, it was given up later because, according to Samuel Kabue of the Ecumenical Disability Advocates Network-WCC, the term was only understood within ecumenical family and especially in churches and organizations closely related to WCC.[4] Some arguments against this term were also made by the people it refers to, with a sentiment that the term has its hazard to neglect their suffering situation. They argue: "who is in this case not differently abled in the entire world population and if we all are, who then does the term refer to?".[5] These arguments against this inclusive terminology are of course non theological. The suggestion to abandon the usage of "differently abled" and to opt for the terms of "persons with disabilities" or "people with disabilities" is by no mean a satisfactory choice.

Of course we have to take into account the hopes and desires of those postnatal "disabled" for healing and to be treated justly in the society. However, the term itself is a social construction of discrimination made by the so call "able" people. You should attempt in vain pursuing justice by accepting a discriminatory status.

Starting from a medical model World Health Organization has defined the disability as: "The disadvantage or restriction of activity caused by contemporary social organization which takes no or little account of people who have physical impairments and thus excludes them from participation in the mainstream of social activities".[6] In another words the concept of disability has to do with accessibility of participation. Thus, social construction has not only construct the identity of a group of people, but it constructs also an environment to prevent them to participate. The issue involves a critical matter of "power", an exclusive power that majority people exercised to preclude heterogeneous individuals. This dominant superior power of exclusion hence needs to be examined and dealt with theologically.

III Revisiting the Christian concept of *imago Dei*

In ancient time when human interactions were limited within family and tribes, urbanization and industrialization have not been developed, and technologies were still preliminary, accessibility was not causing much problem to the so called disabled people; in some primitive cultural circumstance, they were considered divine and capable to serve as spiritual (psychic) medium to proclaim and prophesy. Enlightenment movement – which represented civilization development in both material aspect of science and technology and spiritual aspect of upholding rational thinking – is considered one of key impacts to divide people into normal and healthy, over against the sick and the disabled. People who were physically and mentally retarded were considered as lower in the order of evolution.[7] The eugenic movement considered such people as a hindrance to the growth and perfection of the human community.[8]

Inherited the idea of the "holiness" nature of God, the Hebrew bible, particularly the Leviticus "Holiness Code" (Lev 21:16-23), has strongly opposed for the "blemished" to serve the priesthood, and Jesus in the New Testament instead evidently declares the moral innocence of the disabled person (John 9:1-11). According to the stories told by the Gospels, in his ministry Jesus often responded to the people of infirmity with compassion. He healed many kinds of diseases and recovered their impairments to restore their health. These stories have encouraged Christian church worldwide to launch significant contributions for human health through its medical mission. The Christian ministry for disabled people has been part of this movement. However, towards the end of his life, Jesus has taken a revolutionary step to let himself become blemish by submitted himself to be crucified on the cross and wounded his body (John 19:31-37). The son of God became, to say, "disabled" challenging the traditional doctrine of the image of God that has been one-sidedly stressing its nature of divinity and perfection. Traditional figure of God is incapable to suffer and to accommodate imperfection and defects.

This image of God defined as divinity and perfection, which disgraced the infirmity and weakness, cannot be the integrated image of God that is confessed to be the creator of the world. Theological speaking, if God has a particular image, we can only know it through God's work of creation; though the creation story emphasized that only human being was created to reflect the image of God, yet there is no biblical passage to define an archetype body of humanity. God's creation was various and deep. The first creation story witnessed that God saw all the creatures were good and "each according its kind" (Gen 1:3), there was no sole standard of physical shape of limbs, organs and even degrees of intellect. All are good in their kind. Therefore all creatures enjoyed their being free and life flourishing in God's world. There are birds without hands, snakes without legs, fishes live under waters and some creatures are without eyes, yet none of them could be called disabled. Among the numerous creatures there are discrepancy and distinction, in colour, in shape, sizes and aptness. Some are strong some are weak, some are fast some are slow, some are ingenious some are stagnant. But no moral implication can be attributed to these differences. On the contrary, the weaker parts are mostly critical to the whole and deserved more cherishing. As Paul used the body as a metaphor to advise the church of Corinthians for unity and solidarity, he says:

> [12] For just as the body is one and has many members, and all the members of the body, though many, are one body, so it is with Christ. [13] ... The eye cannot say to the hand, "I have no need of you," nor again the head to the feet, "I have no need of you." [22] On the contrary, the parts of the body that seem to be weaker are indispensable, [23] and on those parts of the body that we think less honourable we bestow the greater honour, and our unpresentable parts are treated with greater modesty, [24] which our more presentable parts do not require. But God has so composed the

body, giving greater honour to the part that lacked it, [25] that there may be no division in the body, but that the members may have the same care for one another. [26] If one member suffers, all suffer together; if one member is honoured, all rejoice together (1Cor 12:12.21-26).

Disability is thus not to be judged by the shapes or kinds of body, but it is a circumstance confronting environmental inaccessibility that human society created for its own species. Ability is mostly postnatal developed through living beings interacting with their environments. No people are born disabled in nature, but some disadvantaged have been prevented to freely employ or developing their abilities, and meanwhile being disgraced and categorized as disabled. Therefore it is a human exercise of corrupt powers and advantages that creates an environment preventing different people to freely access and to live with, which is the matter of injustice and hegemonic: this demands theological critiques and to seek ways to overcome it. From a theological perspective, thus, it is urgent and necessary, we should get rid with the discriminatory concept of disability. If we take in consideration the argument that the disadvantage of the "disabled" needs to be paid attention to, and that we cannot despise the pain and unjust treatments experienced in the society, I would suggest the term of "Discriminated Differently Abled" or "Disadvantaged Differently Abled" (DDA) as a subject for discourses.

The studies on "Discriminated Differently Abled" issue have challenged the traditional doctrine of *imago Dei*. The nature of God the creator is of course rich in abilities and skills, which traditionally it has been described by the concept of omnipotence, omniscience, and omnipresence. It is, however, proper of the Christian confession about God the creator that God is also rich in compassion. The divine love of God that is the centre message of the Gospel has witnessed by the vulnerability of the same abled God, who suffered to have the only beloved Son to be crucified, injured and despised.

IV Rethinking the nature of mission from the "Discriminated Differently Abled" concern

As mentioned above, Christian community, starting from its traditional doctrine of divine nature of God, has derived a history of devaluing attitudes towards "Discriminated Differently Abled" people. In her article titled "sacramental bodies", Nancy Eiesland discussed the different marginalizing attitudes that churches have in regard to people with disabilities. She suggests that the church "has too long provided the ideological funding and charitable practices to people with disabilities which results in marginalization".[9]

Christian mission inherited from the models of Jesus' ministry in first century Palestine, has developed three aspects of projects, namely: prophetic witness, priestly Service and servant king caring. And thus "proclaiming justice, peace and creation integrity" (prophetically), "evangelization, faith nurturing and church planting" (priestly) as well loving care such as "education, medication and charity activities" are implemented to reflect church's identity and mission. However, the issue of "Discriminated Differently Abled" has for too long time been taken for granted by the Christian tradition and people as an object to be put under the third category of caring ministry: intentionally or unintentionally they have ignored the prophetic aspect of the issue. It is imperative to revisit the Christian mission of Charity under this challenge of rediscover the reality of so called "disability".

Christian charity has been lauded as a virtue of Christian mission; however, as C.D. Batson has pointed out, "it has wounded very many persons with disabilities as they have been used to perpetuate acts of charity or during the promotion of pro-social behaviour which is aimed at benefiting other people rather than promoting one's own well-being".[10] Psychologists have pointed out that helping others is personally beneficial, by self-awards or such as positive feedback for being kind, even though without external rewards. Not to say that most of the charity foundations have been doing that annually, as they were required to give away large sums as the condition of tax exemption.[11] Church and its mission have to transform themselves in order to gain back their credibility.

V Re-imaging the Reign of God through transformation of Churches and Communities to Inclusive Churches and Communities

Church is a community shaped by Jesus' movement. In another words, Church in its original implication was a community of people who were selected and invited to join Jesus' new initiative of "God's reign (kingdom)" movement. Jesus' movement was a radical project under the Roman Empire. There were various ministries that Jesus had performed among his activities: he spread the Word of God, cared for poor, women and marginalized, as well healed sickness. But most of all, he prophetically declared an alternative hope to hopeless people and those who were oppressed, exploited and discriminated under the hegemonic power of Roman Empire. His teaching on the mount has promised to the excluded people that a genuine happiness is assured to those that are suffering under the unjust worldly power and structure, merely if they are willing to accept the Reign of God (Matthew 5:1-11).

Contrary to the worldly empire of Rome, in which the followers of Jesus were treated insignificantly and peripheral, Jesus in his mission inauguration address on the mount has announced that there is an alternative empire or kingdom that is ruled by God and is promised to be owned by this group of people who were/are ignored and excluded by their societies. He particularly points out the nature of this alternative Kingdom (Empire) of God in his teaching of Beatitudes, saying:[12]

> ³ "Blessed are the poor in spirit, for theirs is the kingdom of heaven. ...
> ...
> ¹⁰ "Blessed are those who are persecuted for righteousness' sake, for theirs is the kingdom of heaven.
> If Church is truly the community of Jesus' movement, it cannot be a community *against* the poor, marginalized or persecuted; it is even nor a community *for* them, but *is including them and belong to them.*

VI Inclusive Church and inclusive Christian mission

Almost in all societies, the "Discriminated Differently Abled" persons suffered by cultural taboos and prejudices, social stigmas and exclusion, and even religious condemnation and theological depreciation. They are often considered inferior and being treated unjustly to disable them from normal lives. Yet churches remain silent in their prophetic ministries, and instead have one-sided implemented charity programs to contain and categorize this group of marginalized people. Though not to denial the necessity of churches' caring for the disadvantaged people, this blindness to the marginalization caused by their own action has caused the churches losing their important rule as an instrument of liberation, but became one of the places where people experienced discrimination and exclusion.

In the case of "Discriminated Differently Abled", cultural prejudice and social discrimination create a cycle of disability, poverty and marginalization. Should the church continually employ its traditional doctrine of "image of God" and "Christology" to stress ability and perfection, Christian attitude towards the "Discriminated Differently Abled" will continue classifying them negative and inferior. It's time for the churches to revisit boldly their diakonia through contributions made by "Discriminated Differently Abled": they are created in the *imago Dei* and exist to display the work of the Father of Jesus Christ (John 9:1-3). The issue can to be taken as an issue of justice and to be dealt with as a prophetic concern, and as well we have to work for a total repentance and conversion. Only when conscientized activists and churches are prepared to challenge the *status quo* in the spirit of disinterested love, the concept of church and mission will be transformed to a more relevant one for all God's people.

Disabled people are differently abled people. They construct a diversity, which needs to be accepted in love and empathy. They are a part of the creation, the human family.[13] They are part of the world created by God and subject of our societies; we should not take them as object of church's charity programs. We need to make the church an inclusive space "not by holding special events in which the non-disabled allow the disabled to participate, but by constructing fully integrated environments in which all have access as equally as possible."[14] Inclusive church demands affirmation and recognition of the equal rights of the "Discriminated Differently Abled" persons, which means accepting them as active subjects, talented and creative in their own capacities for ministry.[15]

Notes

1. Samuel Kabue, Disability, Church and Society: A Historical and Sociological Perspective, *Disability Theology from Asia, A Resource Book For Theological and Religious Studies*, ed. By Anjeline Okola & Wati Longchar, (Inida: PTCA, 2019) p. 24
2. Ibid.,
3. Ibid.
4. Ibid., p. 26.
5. Ibid.
6. Definition made by WHO at 1980, see Samuel Kabue ibid., p. 25.
7. John Samuel, Person with disability in the Hebrew Bible, *A Resource Book For Theological and Religious Studies*, ibid., p. 130
8. Ibid.,
9. Anjeline Okola, Introduction, "EDAN-WCC Initiatives on Inclusive Church and Communities", *Disability Theology From Asia: A Resource Book For Theological and Religious Studies* ibid., p. xv. See Nancy L. Eiesland, The disabled God: Toward a Liberatory Theology of Disability (Nashville: Abingdon Press, 1994),p.240
10. C. Daniel Batson, " Altruism and prosocial behaviour", in *The Handbook of Social Psychology*, eds. D.T. Gibert, S.T. Fiske, & G. Lindzey (New York, NY, US: McGraw-Hill, 1998), pp. 282-316
11. Okola, *Disability Theology From Asia*, p. xvi.
12. See Matthew 5.1-11
13. Martin Adhikary, Disability and social justice in Islamic Societies in Asia, *Disability Theology From Asia*, ibid., p. 53.
14. Anjeline Okola, ibid., p. xix.
15. Limatula Longkumer, Ministry Among Persons with Disabilities, *Disability Theology From Asia*, ibid., pp. 382-383.

Part Three: Rethinking Humanity

Rethinking Charity

ANNE MASTERS

The charity model of disability has been soundly rejected by individuals with disabilities in favour of one that emphasizes rights and empowerment. Although good to be rejected, models based on rights and empowerment also have limits, as evidenced by the ongoing transgression of the rights of persons with disabilities. I will suggest that the rejected model of charity is actually a perversion of it, and then argue for rethinking charity, based on human dignity, within the framework provided by Catholic Social Teaching. Such a model can actually address what rights and empowerment does not.

> If you acknowledge your possessions as coming from God, is He unjust because He apportions them unequally? Why are you rich when another is poor, unless it be that you may have the merit of a good stewardship, and he the reward of patience?[1]

The above quote of St. Basil claims that God makes some people poor and weak to provide the wealthy and strong with opportunities for service, so they may become more like Christ. This thinking is the source of what is referred to as the charity model of disability, which is generally maligned and rejected. Pope Benedict XVI also notes it "has been and continues to be misconstrued and emptied of meaning, with the consequent risk of being misinterpreted, detached from ethical living... ."[2] Such problems with the charity model have contributed to the development of one based on rights. While I agree with the issues in the charity model, I question if the rights-based argument per se is sufficient to achieve its purpose. Looking into the historical development of charity may provide insight into where it lost its way and suggest possibilities for recovery. Is something is to be gained by rethinking charity? That is the question I will pursue in this article.

Models provide a framework to interpret the dynamics or beliefs about a particular issue. Concerning disabilities, the different models provide a particular lens on the human experience of disability, that is reflected in its name. The existence of a model does not make its positions true, it simply explains them. For example, the medical model presents disability as something to be diagnosed and cured. A model's particular lens then shapes responses, legislation, supports, services and attitudes for and about individuals with disabilities. Focusing on deficits, disability, according to this model is a tragedy. It can only be dealt with through treatment from the medical community to regain wholeness, or through services from charitable organizations and individual to relieve suffering.[3]

I The Problem with Charity

The charity model is based on long standing stereotypes of dependency, sentimentality, and otherness that portray individuals with disabilities more as objects of pity and instruments for others to become better people. This generates stories that discount them as persons who have abilities to contribute to the community. Such was the interpretation of the message from Pope Francis' twitter account promoting On Love in the Family, "People with Disabilities are a gift for the family and an opportunity to grow in love, mutual aid and unity."[4] Pope Francis discussed the family impact of having a child with a within four paragraphs of an apostolic exhortation following the Synod on the Family. He expressed the Church's gratitude that families have affirmed the dignity of life by accepting their child with a disability, he praised the fraternity and affection of siblings toward the "disabled 'little brother or sister,'" and he elevated their need for support from extended family.[5] Within the exhortation, Francis does not identify persons with disabilities as persons of interest who can contribute in varied and different ways, their contributions are bound within their disabilities.

David Perry, an historian, disability rights writer and the father of a boy with Down Syndrome critically responded that the tweet and document "render the disabled family member as object rather than agent, as an opportunity for the able person to demonstrate their goodness rather than a person who might do good themselves, and perpetuate the myth of the disabled individual as eternal child."[6] Kayla Whaley, a writer who has a disability, also strongly rejects this attitude, which "sees us less than human,"[7] and says further, "We are not 'gifts' or 'opportunities' to ~teach abled people about love~."[8] Both Perry and Whaley rightly reject locating the value of individuals with disabilities in instrumental effect on others, which locates the value of a person outside of themselves. This not only denies the innate dignity of every person, but as Hans Reinders correctly points out, the positive response depends on the other person's moral orientation.[9]

Attitudes and opinions about people inform the stories told about them. Stories are both a mechanism to develop understanding and meaning about people and events, as well as to reflect meaning and influence others.[10] Each person tells their story as part of this process, but no one really controls their own story. It is both from direct experiences and second-hand accounts a tapestry woven from the various threads of the different narrators' voices talking about them.[11] These multiple narratives coalesce into a metanarrative, which then impacts how people are treated, how they understand themselves and what opportunities they may have for relationships and participation within their life. Stories inform individual and community identities.[12] Therefore, the stories told about people matter.

However well-intentioned someone may be with such statements as Pope Francis made, the charity narrative about disability perpetuates the status quo of systemic structures that maintains the dependency of persons with disabilities on the beneficence of others.[13] Such dependency lacks any predictability or reliability, but more importantly, it ignores the innate value of individuals with disabilities.

II Rights vs Charity

A rights-based model of disability rejects the deficit-based, patronizing principles of the medical and charity models. Taking its cue from the civil rights movement, it is based on individual rights, to oppose the transgressions against persons with disabilities. Despite legislative support in some countries and international agreements about rights of individuals with disabilities, such success continues to be elusive. The UN Convention of the Rights of Persons with Disabilities (CRPD) is a common international reference point. Tara Melish of the United States and Giampiero Griffo of Italy both argue for the importance of state ratification of the agreement, with specific concerns for their respective countries. Melish argues that it would strengthen the Americans with Disabilities Act.[14] Griffo bemoans the CRPD's limited effectiveness, because of the number of countries that still have not passed supportive legislation, even though they ratified it.[15]

Often the specifics details lack clarity, by stipulating what is 'reasonable' or by following elongated time lines. Rights have been important to identify the structural forces which discriminate individuals with disabilities.[16] Yet to truly be successful, more complete cooperation is required from the community. However, attitudes and emotions cannot be legislated.[17] Rights, like charity in its current manifestation, seems to similarly depend on the inclinations and beliefs of others, even if in different ways. Honouring the rights of individuals requires clear stipulation in the law, and ready agreement by the community, including the community providers intended to support their progress.

What would be a more helpful way to understand disability that includes a built in framework which respects all individuals with disabilities as persons of interest and concern, rather than objects for the benefit of others? In the words of Perry, is there a theology on disability that "would open pathways to witness and embrace our shared humanity, regardless of the functioning of our bodies and minds, and understand that all of us need the opportunities to be both actors and be acted upon as we pursue a good life in our communities"?[18]

III Rethinking Charity

The charity model as it stands undermines respect for human dignity, which all of Catholic Social Teaching is based on. But what if charity has been misconstrued? Going back in time may help to understand developments today that grew out of earlier events. This will not be an exhaustive historical expose, but enough to notice shifting trends that may suggest emergent patterns associated with questions of today. Because the Hebrew Scriptures and culture influenced the Christians charity tradition received from Christ, it is important to consider the Gospel in light of its Jewish roots as well.

Rethinking Charity

Jewish practices for charity prior to the fourth century, C.E. were concerned with attending to physical sustenance needs, as well as for personal and social impacts of poverty. They were organized to maintain the privacy of the individuals served and do away with public begging.[19] This served both respect for persons receiving charity and also the good of the community. However, during the fourth century, both Jewish and Christian ecclesial charity structures began to consolidate economic, political and religious power.[20] As Christianity and the Jewish Diaspora spread, they encountered Greco-Roman philosophies about wealth, poverty and social order that lacked an appreciation for Yahweh's covenantal relationship with the people of Israel, and its underlying concern about people who are marginalized and vulnerable.[21] Over time such influence can be discerned in Christian practice of almsgiving as acts of kindness became oriented for personal redemption, rather than kindness growing for the good of the community.

Another branch of charitable activity also was developing around this same time in monasteries. St. Benedict of Nursia, popularly considered the "Father of Monasticism," was indirectly very influential in the next turn of charity under consideration. From the beginning monastic spirituality was firmly grounded in Scripture with the practice of *lectio divina,* which informed their life in community. Preferred Scripture passages highlighted the importance of providing hospitality, identifying with strangers, being concerned for people who are vulnerable and in need, and recognizing that Christ is present in every person.[22] Within the monastic system, the monastery is the *house of God* because of the "perfect presence of Christ as all in all, in the one who welcomes and in the one who is received," which is captured in the metaphor of "the two faces of Christ." One opens and gives; the other knocks and makes himself a beggar. In this we see the role of beggar as a metaphor applied to whoever was receiving. To the monks in Benedict's day, Christ was present in the Abbot, the monks, the guests and those who were sick or poor.[23]

Charity according to Benedict was rooted in holy obligation, and it was to be done with humility within relationships and acts of service, amongst the monks and between the monks and guests. Someone's need was the guide for distribution, not rank or status, though their condition in life was considered when providing assistance.[24] So far, it is difficult to see any connection between monastic tradition of charity and today's problematic charity model, which lacks any sense of mutuality or sense of Christ's presence in the person receiving charity.

Benedict's monastery wasn't the only option in its day, nor the predominant one until outside events changed its course. When Charlemagne unified the Catholic Church in Europe within a feudal society based on previous imperial models, it combined ecclesial and political structures to bind the empire, "ruling through 'a managerial aristocracy' composed of powerful laymen, bishops and great abbots."[25] *Benedict's Rule* was promoted and adopted as the ideal to organize the charitable activities of the Empire and the Church. Though its simplicity was original appealing, the amount of discretion it privileged to the abbot was problematic within this new structure. Though the monastery still was a place for the monks to seek God through prayer, asceticism and liturgical service, it was also "an organ of the Christian state" with all its implied privileges and obligations.[26] This new identity and structure was the first change during this time which impacted Christian charity tradition.

The second change was the standardization on vernacular language in society with its consequent reduced use of Latin. Though Latin remained in liturgy and prayer, this restricted most access and understanding to clergy and monks, and thus initiated a new fissure within the spirituality of charity. The monks were increasingly involved with academic work transcribing and writing, leaving little time to care for travellers and vulnerable people. This would require a new group of workers to do the work of and for the monastery, which was accomplished by establishing *conversi,* an order of laymen admitted to religious life. Their identity was a bit confused within the order, not really equivalent to today's religious brother. They were typically uneducated and didn't speak Latin or participate in the liturgical life of the monastery. This meant that those devoted to prayer were no longer connected with works of charity, introducing a hierarchical order of holiness within it, though it was only later that they were considered second class monks of sorts.[27] Through the division of responsibilities, the work of charity was now being assigned to men disconnected from its spiritual roots, in other words, the work of charity was being done without the heart of charity, foreshadowing later developments in its practice. As Fry noted, the integration of monastic charity within the structure of the

Empire would have disastrous consequences.[28]

Benedict's "little book for beginners" became much more complicated and regulated as an arm of the Holy Roman Empire. Whereas *Benedict's Rule* focused on inner orientation, mutuality and trust in the abbot's discernment, and offered flexibility, preference for rubrics and uniformity took over as monasteries grew. They became huge during this time, in comparison to those of Benedict's day. It is not difficult to imagine how the "two faces of Christ" could become lost in the experience of charity.

Recapping this brief review of earlier history of charity highlights some influential shifts that occurred. The roots of Judeo-Christian charity acknowledges that all abilities, possessions and station originate in God, and therefore belong in service to God. Other socio-political developments would continue to shape monasteries throughout the Middle Ages.[29] However, the most influential to this discussion are the two rounds of centralization and institutionalization, in the fourth century and the Carolingian reorganization of the Middle ages. Together, they seem to have ruptured charity's connection with love in its vernacular understanding, making way for the patronizing and self-serving charity model known today. Another round of institutionalization in modern times leaves no trace of charity's basis in God's gratuitous activity amongst humanity through the Spirit.[30] Could knowing these shifts and their causes suggest a possible corrective course? I believe it can.

IV Human Dignity Reclaiming Charity

Reclaiming charity that is based on human dignity would look very different than its corrupted model. Catholic Social Teaching provides this basis, which respects the dignity of every person, who is created in the image of God. Charity, caritas, is both its central value and animating force. Locating someone's value in providing others the opportunity to grow in love, or become better people, misses the presence of Christ in them, thus undermining the two faces of Christ that was so integral to monastic charity. To move beyond the subverted practice of charity, Pope Benedict suggests that "truth needs to be sought, found and expressed within the "economy" of charity,"[31] The process of doing charity matters. In this way, charity, formed by truth, moves beyond sentimentality and emptiness, it moves beyond outdated stereotypes and prejudices, and finds new solutions as it unites knowledge and practice for human and community flourishing. The ability to do this, which requires the ability to be concerned beyond one's self comes through activity of the Spirit (Rom 5:5).32

This concern for human dignity requires that every person should have access to the basic things required for a truly human life: food, clothing, a home, medical care, education, employment, privacy, and respect, participating in family, social and political life, having diverse relationships, exercising ones rights and responsibilities, and even making mistakes.33 This is a major outcome of Vatican II, which continues to be affirmed in papal teaching and statements of bishop conferences, so the Church may respond to the changing needs of human society.

Catholic Social Teaching does not proclaim what would be nice to do. It states what it is required to do. The Church as an organization and in its individual members, needs to collaborate in the world to eliminate the existence and effects of poverty and injustice for all people. Taken seriously, it can provide the framework for a renewed understanding of charity within its three organizational principles of solidarity, concern for the common good and subsidiarity. Solidarity means to feel the experiences of others as one's own (1 Cor 12:26). Concern for the common good considers the needs of the most vulnerable as part of the community's well-being. Such concern counters liberal society's singular focus on individualism and individual rights.34 Subsidiarity means to empower growth and development through participation, rather than dependency. The move beyond dependency that Catholic Social Teaching promotes here still acknowledges the interdependent and social nature of human beings, rather than staunch individualism and independence of liberal society. This is a critical area of concern for individuals with profound or more involved disabilities, due to their typical isolation in segregated settings. Friendships, a natural part of human life, cannot be legislated nor dictated. They evolve through proximity and interaction within a sphere of mutual respect.

The call to action for recovering the doing of charity is to recover mutuality, in 'the two faces of Christ,' rather than hiding behind programmatic structures.35 As Karl Rahner says, "we cannot do anything else than see our own fate in that of our neighbour."36 With authentic

Rethinking Charity

charity, there is the realization that all are called to "journey in community side by side with others" in the details of daily life.37 The ability to do this comes from God's grace to transform indifferent and fearful hearts into hearts that are willing to become entangled in others' lives.[38]

Notes

1. Francis L.B. Cunningham, *The Christian Life*, Eugene, OR: Wipf & Stock Publishers, 2010, 420. Google Books. https://books.google.com/books?id=d3VMAwAAQBAJ.
2. Pope Benedict XVI, Charity in Truth, *Caritas in Veritate*. Vatican City: Libreria Editrice Vaticana, 2009, par. 2, Kindle.
3. David Johnstone, *An Introduction to Disability Studies: Second Edition*, with a new introduction by the author, Great Britain: Routledge, 2001, 22-27, 103-106. For more information on different models of disability, this book is a good primer on the development of the different models of disability.
4. Pope Francis, „Tweet-People with Disabilities Are a Gift," Pope Francis @Pontifex, Posted 9 April 2016 4:00 AM at https://twitter.com/pontifex/status/718710082406473728. [9 April 2016]
5. Pope Francis, *The Joy of Love (Amoris Laetitia): On Love in the Family*, Vatican City, Libreria Editrice Vaticana, 2015, par. 47, 195, 97, Kindle. An apostolic exhortation following the Synod on the Family.
6. David Perry, „'Amoris Laetitia' Reflects Narrow View of Disabled Persons," CRUX, 4 June 2016, at http://www.cruxnow.com/church/2016/04/12/amoris-laetitia-reflects-narrow-view-of-disabled-persons. [13 May 2016]
7. Kayla Whaley, „Disabled People Are People: A Message to the Pope," in Telling your followers to view us as objects that exist for the edification of abled people, tells them we're less than human, @Pontifex., ed. @PunkinOnWheels 9 April 2016 8:53 AM. [13 May 2016]
8. „Disabled People Are People: A Message to the Pope," in The Pope tweeted about disabled people as gifts and opportunities for abled people. I responded. Then the pushback to my call out started @PunkinOnWheels 9 April 2016 8:44 AM.. Disabled people are PEOPLE. Full stop. We are not „gifts" or „opportunities" to ~teach abled people about love~, ed. @PunkinOnWheels (2016); ibid. [13 May 2016]
9. Hans S. Reinders, *Receiving the Gift of Friendship*, Grand Rapids: Wm. B. Eerdmans Publishing, 2008, 280-283.
10. Herbert Anderson and Edward Foley, *Mighty Stories, Dangerous Rituals*, San Francisco: Jossey-Bass, 2007, chapters 1 and 2, Kindle.
11. John Swinton, Harriet Mowat, and Susannah Baines, „Whose Story Am I? Redescribing Profound Intellectual Disability in the Kingdom of God," *Journal of Religion, Disability & Health* 15.1 (2011): 5-19, here 11-12.
12. Anderson and Foley, Mighty Stories, chapters 1 and 2.
13. Giampiero Griffo, "Models of disability, ideas of justice, and the challenge of full participation". *Modern Italy*, 19(2), 147-159. doi:10.1080/13532944.2014.910502148.
14. Tara J. Melish, „The UN Disability Convention: Historic Process, Strong Prospects,

and Why the U.S. Should Ratify." *Human Rights Brief* 14, no. 2 (2007): 43-46.
15. Griffo, „Models of Disability," 150-156.
16. Johnstone, *Disability Studies*, 31.
17. Hans Reinders, "What's Wrong with Charity? Considerations for a Modern Travesty of Christian Ethics," Translated by Hans Reinders, in *Say What's Up, Try Exploratory Ethics,* Ceremony in Honor of Hans G. Ulrich, (eds), Gerard den Hertog, Stefan Heuser, Marco Hofheinz and Bernd Wannenwetsch, Leipzig: Evangelical Publishing House, 2017, 135-160, here. (Author's copy, p. 3); Hans S. Reinders, *Receiving the Gift of Friendship*, 138-150. .
18. David Perry, "Pope Francis Needs To Do More Than Kiss The Disabled," CRUX, 14 June 2016, at https://cruxnow.com/vatican/2016/06/14/pope-francis-needs-kiss-disabled [14 June 2016].
19. Gregg E Gardner, *The Origins of Organized Charity in Rabbinic Judaism*, Cambridge University Press, 2015, 8-10, Kindle.
20. For more information about these parallel developments in charity, see Greeg E. Gardner, *The Origins of Organized Charity in Rabbinic Judaism*, Cambridge, Cambridge University Press 2015; and Helen Rhee, *Loving the Poor, Saving the Rich: Wealth, Poverty, and Early Christian Formation*, Grand Rapids, MI: Baker Books, 2012. Kindle. Both authors provide extensive background about the views on poverty, wealth, and social justice in Jewish texts and Christian texts in Jesus' day and contrast it with Greco-Roman philosophies. Both books provide helpful insight into this area, including suggestions for implications on Patristic conversations on charity.
21. Rhee, Loving the Poor, Saving the Rich, 27.
22. Mayeul de Dreuille, O.S.B., *The Rule of Saint Benedict: A Commentary in Light of World Ascetic Traditions*, Mahwah, NJ: Paulist Press, 2002, 316, 20, 18, 19. Among these were Lev 19:34, Acts 4:32-35, Lk 14:13-14, Mt 10:40-41, and Mt 25:35-43. The prophetic texts: 2 Sam 12: 1-6; 2 Kings 4:13; Amos 5, etc. The importance of hospitality in Lev 19:34; Deut 10: 17-19.
23. de Dreuille, *The Rule of Saint Benedict: A Commentary*, 331-333. Timothy Fry, OSB, ed. RB 1980: The Rule of St. Benedict in English, Collegeville, MN: Liturgical Press, 1982. Rules 2:2; 4:21; 5.2; 53:1; 72:11.
24. Fry, RB 1980: Latin and English, 233; RB 1980: in English. Though this is woven throughout, particularly helpful examples are Rules 4:1-78; 7:1-70; 71:1-9; 72:1-12; 31:1-19; 32:1-5; 34:1-7; 53:1-23.
25. Roger Haight, SJ, *Christian Community in History*, New York, London: Continuum, 2004, 271.
26. Fry, RB 1980: Latin and English, 123.
27. Fry, RB 1980: Latin and English, 128-29. The *conversi* referenced here are separate from another use of *conversi* which developed in the 11st century within Cistercian monasteries motivated by penance, and/or piety, which Fry discusses on p. 418.
28. Fry, RB 1980: Latin and English, 123.
29. Fry, RB 1980: Latin and English, 131. Such as moves from feudal to urban life that significantly changed monasteries' economics, developing clericalism in the Church, political changes, the Black Death, the Hundred Years' War, as well as evolving problems within monasteries.
30. Reinders, "What's Wrong with Charity?, 2-3, 14-15.
31. Pope Benedict XVI, *Caritas in Veritate*, par. 2.
32. Pope Benedict XVI, *Caritas in Veritate*, par. 3, 4, 30-32, 5.

33. Council Fathers of Vatican II, „Pastoral Constitution on the Church in the Modern World," [*Gaudium et Spes*], ed. Austin Flannery, trans. Ambrose McNicholl, OP, Paul Lennon, OCarm, and Austin Flannery, OP, Vatican Council II: Constitutions, Decrees, Declarations: The Basic Sixteen Documents. A Completely Revised Translation in Inclusive Language, Collegeville, MN: Liturgical Press, 1996, par. 23-28, 40; USCCB, „Economic Justice for All: Catholic Social Teaching and the U.S. Economy," Washington, DC: United States Conference of Catholic Bishops, 1986, reprint, 1997, par. 77, 79-80, USCCB at http://www.usccb.org/upload/economic_justice_for_all.pdf [22 July 2019]; USCCB, „A Century of Social Change: A Common Heritage, a Continuing Challenge," Washington, DC: United States Conference of Catholic Bishops, 1990, 1-2, http://www.usccb.org/beliefs-and-teachings/what-we-believe/catholic-social-teaching/upload/A-Century-of-Social-Heritage.pdf [19 February 2019].
34. Michael J. Himes, S.J. and Kenneth R. Himes, O.F.M., Fullness of Faith: The Public Significance of Theology, New York/Mahwah, NJ: Paulist Press, 1993, 63-73.
35. Pope Benedict XVI, *Caritas in Veritate*, par. 7
36. Karl Rahner, "Christology Today?" *Theological Investigations*: Vol. IV, translated by Margaret Kohl, New York: Crossroad, 1981, 24-38, here 32.
37. Pope Francis,*Gaudete Et Exsultate*, Vatican City: Liberia Editrica Vaticana, 2018, par.141at http://w2.vatican.va/content/francesco/en/apost_exhortations/documents/papa-francesco_esortazione-ap_20180319_gaudete-et-exsultate.pdf [10 April 2018]
38. Pope Francis, *Gaudete Et Exsultate*, par. 139-146.

Living Together in the Household of God: From a Person with Disabilities Perspective

STEPHEN ARULAMPALAM

The world we are living in is full of wounds; in this context, we are called by the wounded God to share his love through our words and deeds to the wounded people in order to create equality, justice and peace. In this article I will specifically focus on the missiology for the persons with disabilities.

My personal wounded experience and the experience of my family challenged me to work towards the persons with disabilities. In the wounded world, persons with disabilities are socially, politically, culturally and economically excluded in the form of verbal, psychological and physical, in the church and in the society in Sri Lanka.

In this article I will define who a disable is, and how they are excluded by the society and church and how missiology can heal the wounds of the persons with disabilities. In my new missiology, I will include; the wounded God, Blind Christology, New spirituality, Re-interpreting miracles of Jesus and re-reading the hymns and proverbs from the perspective of persons with disabilities. This will help the people with disabilities to live together with all people in the house hold of God. I will then make suggestions and recommendations for the church.

Living Together in the Household of God

I Introduction
I'm Arulampalam Stephen, attached to the Theological College of Lanka Pillimathalawa in the centre part of Sri Lanka. When I was 9 months I had fever, doctor gave me a wrong medicine that affected my nerves, due to the reason my sight started to decrease. Now I'm enjoying the life of blindness. In this context, even though I have applied to ministry immediately my secondary studies, church did not give a positive answer to me, because it was a new issue for the church as well. Some or rather, they accepted me later on; in the midst of everything in 1995 my house was bombed by the armies in Jaffna (northern part of Sri Lanka); due to that, my father lost his right leg and became a disable person as well; and also my mother is still living with some shell pieces in her body. She got to become a disable. Immediately after my ordination, I was appointed as a chaplain at school for deaf and blind in Kaithady (Jaffna), where I was able to listen to the stories of many people. During this period, due to the war, number of people became disable: my personal experience and the experience of the other people pushed me to create a theology of disability in my own context.

II What is Ecumenism?
"Oikoumene" is derived from the Greek word *oikein*, to inhabit. Carrying the meaning of "inhabited earth" or "the whole world", the term has been used since Herodotos (5th century). A comprehensive understanding of oikoumene would include both churchly and worldly, and spiritual and missionary aspects. The concept of oikoumene extends beyond the fellowship of Christians and churches to include the whole human community within the whole creation. The calling of the ecumenical movement is to transform the oikoumene ('inhabited earth') into the oikos ('living household') of God.

Ecumenism is understood differently among the churches of the reformation: for many protestant majority churches 'ecumenical' refers to external relations with churches in other countries; for those living among a diversity of denominations, 'ecumenical' means the coming together of churches; for many, the ecumenical movement expresses itself in Christian concern for justice and peace in a world community. The ecumenical movement in Sri Lanka draws together Roman Catholics, protestant churches, and younger churches in the attempt to become one body of Christ.

According to the Roman catholic ecumenist Bernard Lambert, the ecumenical movement is one of the great religious phenomena of our times; no Christian denomination has remained completely outside it. A new reality is coming into being. There is a wind blowing, which is the wind of the Spirit, and its direction is towards new beginnings. In this paper I would like to focus doing the theology of disability within the context of oikoumene.

III Who is Disabled?

Generally people refer this community as handicapped/disabled people, mentally retarded (mentally challenged), differently abled people, people with disabilities and crippled, wheelchair users. One billion people, or 15% of the world's population, experience some form of disability. About 80% of persons with disabilities live in developing countries, according to the UN Development Programme (UNDP). The World Bank estimates that 20% of the world's poorest people are disabled, and tend to be regarded in their own communities as the most disadvantaged. About 70% of people living in poverty worldwide are *female*! Women with disabilities are more likely to be poorer, less healthy, and more vulnerable to abuse than men with disabilities or non-disabled women. Women with disabilities are recognized to be doubly disadvantaged, experiencing *exclusion* on account of their gender and their disability. Ecumenism has its goal into this: that all members of society enjoy equal rights and opportunities and are able to fully participate in civil, political, economic, social and cultural spheres of life.

In Universal declaration of Human Rights, article 23 (1) states that: "Everyone has the right to work, to free choice of employment, to just and favourable conditions of work and protection against unemployment." National Policy on Disability for Sri Lanka promotes and protects the rights of people who have disability in the spirit of social justice. They will have opportunities for enjoying a full and satisfying life and for contributing to national development with their knowledge, experience and particular skills and capabilities as equal citizens of Sri Lanka. In Sri Lanka, the school of deaf and blind in Kaithady (Northern part of

Sri Lanka), the school for deaf and blind in Rathmalana Colombo, the "Valvagam" (giving life) in Jaffna are the education centres who are concern about the education of the disabled children. Deaf Link Methodist Church and Siva Boomi (Land of Shiva) are the institutions concerned on the empowerment of children. House of Hope in Vavuniya and the New Light Centre are concerned about the employment of the people.

IV Disability and Religion

Asia is unique with different religions and faiths. Religious life is so significant to millions of individuals across the cultures. Generally speaking, religions have ignored people with disabilities. Religions play a major role in the perception of the people, in the perceptions of the disabled about themselves, and that of others, in a world that is heavily influenced by the religion.[1] Symbols that are being used in the religion are culturally rooted.

Symbols that become oppressive power symbols have to be moved to empowering symbols which are vital for any marginalized community. Nancy Eieslands argues people with disabilities need symbols that affirm the dignity of life not only to other people with disabilities, but also to able-bodied persons.[2] Religions are supposed to fight for the justice for the disabled, but it means to become agents of charity and compassion.

V Disability and church

Churches in Sri Lanka engage with the marginalized. The charitable projects and mission outreach projects have evolved from the vision to serve people with disabilities. But churches often ignore the struggles of the disabled. In Nancy Eiesland's opinion, for the disabled, church is like a 'city on a hill': physically inaccessible and socially inhospitable.[3] Church incarnates the disabled God through Jesus who embodied a commitment to justice, who challenged all structures. The integral mission becomes possible only when the voice of the disabled people are heard, their experiences are honoured and their gifts are allowed to flourish.[4]

Disabled God is a God who became disabled during the time of the crucifixion and also we remember this same God during the time of Holy Communion. He is a God who remains with a brokenness and scars (John 20:27). The task of the ecumenical movements is to side with the disabled to have a right space within the church, not to passively support the structure of the society that alienates the disabled.

VI Biblical understanding of disability

There was no clear classification of able–disabled people in the old testament. The understanding of disablement in old and new testament tradition is based on the socio-political context of Judaeo-Christian world. Disablement is simply considered as a punishment for sin Genesis 19:11 describes disablement as punishment for people from Sodom, who attempted to have relationship with the messengers of the Lord. Exodus 4:11 says God is the source of disablement: "who makes him (the human) dumb or deaf, Is it not I, the Lord?", and in Leviticus law, infirmity and disabilities are associated with holiness code.[5] Disability was considered as a mark of impurity or blemish. Leviticus warns that no one who had blemish shall draw near... or a man with a defect in his body... shall not come near to offer the Lord's offering (Leviticus 21: 18-21).[6] At the same time there are instances where God is caring for the disabled. Moses had difficulty in speech, but led the exodus event. David's love towards Mephibosheth is another example of caring for the disabled (2 Samuel 9:9). Thus the Bible does not merely present an exclusive understanding of God and the realities of the disabled, but also gives an inclusive perspective offering human dignity, acceptance and encouragement. These examples give us an encouraging inclusive understanding of God.

As we come into the New Testament Jesus makes his own such an inclusive interpretation. Good examples would be the Nazareth Manifesto and Jesus' teaching about the kingdom of God: they envisioned an inclusive community that challenges the existing divisions and structures of society (Mark 1:15; Matthew 4:11; Luke 9:60; and John 3:3,5). A special preference for the disabled is visible in Jesus' ministry in Luke's gospel. A similar concern for persons with disabilities is apparent and illustrates that the disabled deserves love and care. In Luke 14:16-24, the poor, the crippled, and the blind were the honoured for the banquets.[7] Jesus performed the miracles when the sick and disabled were excluded from the purity system. The liberating touch of Jesus towards the blind and the lame was a deliberate attempt to counter the existing social order of pure impure divisions. Although the New Testament seems to portray the connection between sin and sickness especially in the miracles, Jesus' attitude towards people with disability must be dealt within the larger framework.

VII The Disabled and Eucharist

Eucharist initiates a fellowship without any discrimination. But for people with disabilities, it is often experience of exclusion and segregation. Nancy Eiesland argues that when the communion is received on the communion rail, people with disabilities are always asked to remain in their respective places and communion would be given in their seats, which is one way of an accommodation for the people with disabilities within the church, but leads the disabled persons to have a solitary experience rather than a corporate experience and are stigmatized of the disabled body from a socialization of Christ' broken body.[8]

Eucharist is the remembrance of the vulnerability and brokenness experience in the Christ event. Jesus invited the disciples to participate in the brokenness and pain by partaking in the communion. (Luke 22:19; Matthew 26:26; Mark 14:22; Luke 22:20; Matthew 26:27-28; Mark 14:23-24)[9] Space and role of persons with disabilities in this experience should not make them feel they are recipients of mercy, but should grant them their rightful space in the eucharist .

VIII Theology from disability perspective

There is a course in the senate of Serampore college, titled "Inclusive community, disability perspective", which shows how theology from a disability perspective is so important in the Sri-lankan academic world. Theology of disabled is practical theology because it deals with the personhood in its vulnerable point, which is not theoretical but practical in every sense, and the personhood of the disabled is routinely questioned.[10] According to Wati Longchar, Christian theology is formulated by able bodied people for the able bodied. Theology from the perspective of persons with disabilities is almost silent in Christian tradition. He says that there is a negative theology towards persons with disabilities constructed by able bodied people.[11]

Theology from perspective of disabled must come from a liberatory voice that initiates dialogue within the community of people and the people living with disabilities must be placed at the speaking centre.[12] The methodology of creating theology for disabled is accessibility. Nancy Eiesland says theological method must provide two way accesses. Persons with disabilities must gain access to the social symbolic life of the church and church must gain access to the social symbolic life of the people with disabilities.[13] This liberatory theology includes a deliberate recognition of lived experience of the persons with disabilities, critical analysis of social theory of disability and institutionalized practices of the church.[14] Liberatory theology of disability is the work of bodily figuration of knowledge. It is not an abstract theory but it is rooted in the bodies, in the actions of disabled and all those who care.[15] Theologizing from the context of people with disability is a response to the justice issue. It cannot be limited to ministerial work.

IX Body politics

The body communicates many things. The body is always crucial in the orders of society. Buddhist insights are significant here to deal with the disabled body. Darla Y. Schumm connects 'impermanence' and 'interdependence' in Buddhism with disability. She argues that *interdependence*[16] means anything in the world that is dependent on the other. Nothing can be seen in isolation. All the disabled or abled people are dependent on all other living beings. It means everyone is mutually connected with one another in a great web of relational interdependence. Another concept is *impermanence*. Buddhism makes clear the notion of wholeness and stableness of body. It teaches that all things are constantly changing. Bodies are always undergoing transformation. Thus Buddhism illuminates abled–disabled, perfect-imperfect, stable or whole body concepts.[17] These concepts are relevant to develop relationally. On the other hand, there is also the concept of 'Karma' in Buddhism which explains disability as a result of Karma (Past action). Thus the suffering of the disabled is connected to the individuals actions of the past.

There is a need of deliberate attention to the physical body. An accessible theological method of Nancy Eiesland necessitates that body be represented as flesh and blood, bones and braces and not simply the rationalized realm of society.[18] This understanding of body evokes the stories of bodies and exploited bodies of disabled. Theological response to disability facilitates a right engagement with the exploited bodies of disabled. It is a political activity because it is a justice issue, which cannot be confined as an act of compassion or under the umbrella of charity. Political action for the disabled will enable to allocate resources and provide benefits and protection to people who need them. John Swindon questions if disability is a political category.[19] Since it is a justice issue, theologizing for disabled is a political intervention.

X Image of God and disability

There is a traditional teaching of the image of God among humans. Patrick McArdle also describes the theological link between *imago Dei* and humanity. This theological construct positions human as a perfect individual who has self reline, rationality and autonomy. These dominant perspectives are missing among the disabled and the image of God in Jesus as individual, male, whole, celibate, without defects of mind or body communicates the theological inconsistency in the nature of God. Therefore he opines that theology should engage with the brokenness of humanity. Which is mirror to humanity and this brokenness is not to be eliminated, but to be celebrated. He introduces 'mutual vulnerability; and 'inter–subjectivity' which has the potential to confront the inconsistencies.[20] McArdle quotes the relational encounter of Immanuel Levinas as that for the one who confronts the other is an essential 'other' who pleads not to be rejected and, ultimately, not to be killed. He says it is in face of the other, one is confronted by his-her own vulnerabilities and frailties.[21] John Swinton travels in a different path: for him there is a shared experience of oppression and there are no individual impairments. All the experiences are melded together in the shared oppression;[22] therefore there is a collective experience for all the disabled.

Samuel George quotes Nancy Eiesland's view that disability is not to be seen as a distortion of the image of God rather human beings reflect the disabled image of God.[23] The image of God is manifested in all humans with dignity and value. It is not dependent on what one accomplishes or contributes, but the dignity and value are permanent which are the essential attributes bestowed by God. Every human life is sacred and every human is to be treated with honour.[24] There is a distortion of value in understanding the image of God.

XI Conclusion

Church needs to witness the vulnerability of God and the God who is disabled through Jesus on the cross. The crucified image as a suffering servant is an empowering and liberating image for the disabled and all those who care for the disabled. The wrong notion of perfection and ability has to be replaced with relational encounters of all human beings. Inclusion and accommodation are not the solutions for accepting the people with disabilities, but remaining of traditional space, envisioning new methodology and mission to have multispaces where all can have equal rights to participate. It is here that the ecumenical churches in Asia along with other communities stand as an alternate ethical community that recognizes the realities of people with disabilities.

Notes

1. A. Brooke Blanks and J. David Smith, "Multiculturalism, Religion, and Disability: Implications for special education practitioners", *Education and Training in Developmental Disabilities* 44/3 (2009) 295.
2. Nancy L. Eiesland, *The Disabled God*, Nashville: Abindon Press, 1994, 92.
3. Eiesland, *The Disabled God*, 20.
4. Nancy L.Eiesland, "Encountering The disabled God", *The Other Side*, September-October, 2002, 15.
5. Fintan B.J. Sheerin, "Jesus and the Portrayal of people with Disabilities in the Scriptures," *Spiritan Horizons*, 8, 2013, 67-68.
6. Samuel N. Kabue," Church and Society's response to disability: Historical and Sociological perspective" A. Wati Longchar and Gordan Cowans, eds. *Doing Theology from disability perspective* (Philipines: ATESEA, 2011), 143.
7. Sam Peedikayil Mathew, "Jesus and persons with Disabilities: A re-reading of the synoptic gospels from a disability perspective", Christopher Rajkumar, ed., Sprouts of disability Theology (Nagpur: NCCI), 50-51.
8. Eiesland, "Encountering", 10.
9 Mathew, " Jesus and persons with Disabilities, 56.
10 Patrick McArdle, " Disability and Relationality: disrupting complacency, entering into vulnerability", Australian eJournal of Theology 17, December 2010, 57.
11 Wati Longchar, 'Engaging Theological Education in context: Focus on persons with Disabilities," Ministerial Formation (WCC) 109, July 2007, 32.
12. Eiesland, *The Disabled God*, 83.
13. Eiesland, *The Disabled God*, 20.
14. Eiesland, *The Disabled God*, 22.
15. Eiesland, *The Disabled God*, 90.
16. Darla Y. Schumm, 'Reimaging Disability," *Journal of Feminist Studies in Religion* 26/2, 133.

17. Schumm, 'Reimaging Disability,", 134.
18. Eiesland, *The Disabled God*, 22.
19. John Swinton, 'From inclusion to belonging: A Practical of Community, Disability and Humanness", *Journal of Religion, Disability and Health*, 16,2012, 188.
20. Patrick McArdle, " Disability and Relationality: disrupting complacency, entering into vulnerability", *Australian eJournal of Theology* 17, December 2010, 58.
21. McArdle," *Disability and Relationality*, 64
22. John Swinton, 'From inclusion to belonging, 175.
23. Samuel George 'Image of God and Disability, stigma and discrimination", Christopher Rajkumar, ed,. *Sprouts of Disability Theology* (Nagpur: NCCI), 64.
24. David W. Anderson, 'Beauty and disability," International Journal of Christianity and Education, 19/3 2015, 185.

Towards Disability Theology in Christianity and Islam

NAEIMEH POURMOHAMMADI

In Christian disability theology, the agenda is that all the theological theses including the knowledge of God, Christology, ecclesiology, and eschatology need to be fundamentally reconsidered. Irrespective of whether or not the theologian is disabled, they put themselves in the position of the people with disability, or ask them questions to learn what understanding and impressions they have of theological elements and teachings, and base theology on those very understandings and impressions.

In Islam, however, nothing like the Christian disability theology has been developed yet. I consider the development of Christian disability theology as a progressive step and a model to be pursued and achieved in Islamic theology. In this article I first give a short introduction to Christian disability theology. Here I show a distant view of a Christian disability theology. Then I provide an account of the Islamic understanding and impression of disability that includes Qur'an and hadith, Islamic sciences, Islamic government, and Islamic culture and civilization, and critique each in separate sections.

I Christian disability theology
a) Weakness of God, Jesus Christ with disability
In 2015, on the margins of the American Academy of Religion's book fair, a book entitled *Theology and Down Syndrome: Reimagining Disability in Late Modernity* grabbed my attention. The image on the book cover was strange: Jesus Christ suffering from Down syndrome, in Mary's arms! This single image conveys "the concept of God" and "the image of

God" in disability theology. It is not extravagant if we imagine that Jesus Christ too was disabled, even sick and suffering and these would detract nothing from his majesty, sacredness and divinity. People with disability are inclined to see Jesus Christ's body as similar to their own, thereby achieving unification with him. They like to build the image of a physical God with a flawed and weak body who has created the disabled in his own shape. Exalted and pure God is increasingly likened, embodied, dependent and communicative so that he can understand the physical limitations of the disabled and empathize with them.

Amos Yong, the author of the above mentioned book has dedicated it to his brother, Mark, who suffers from Down syndrome. Once he asked Mark: "what does it mean that Jesus Christ is our saviour?" "Jesus is my best friend! I have told him. I have said to him that he is my best friend!" Mark answered. On that basis, the book suggests that the model of "Christ as the best friend" takes the place of the model "Christ as the saviour".

b) The church and unification with the disabled Jesus

The church, according to the interpretation of the disability theology, is a community whose members want to get unified not with a perfect and splendid Jesus but with his fractured and crushed body. Jesus is a tormented modest servant of God who, with his injured body, has risen to cure the world. According to this thought, the testimony of Jesus in the church is a testimony of his weakness. This understanding of the church is a re-reading drawing upon the human experience of disability. In this version of the church, what matters is that the physically and cognitively disabled can equally have a part in all the ecclesial beliefs, sacredness, and ceremonies.

c) Resurrection with a disabled body

The important question in disability theology is how the eschatological splendour and majesty of God can be re-pictured in relation to weakness of the disabled human beings, how our eschatological understanding can both take into account the maintenance of the identity of the disabled just as it is, and let them change their identity through the process of salvation, and, so to speak, get healed. In the disability vision, on the one hand, the maintenance of the identity of the disabled is important and their identity should not be presented as flawed and in need of correction and completion. On the other hand, the promises and tidings of the Bible are also important: in the eternal life there will remain no tears or sadness, all the blind and paralyzed and deaf will be healed, all the ugly will become beautiful and all the elderly will become young. A mixture of the two views will lead to the idea that the disabled will be resurrected with their disabled bodies, though the state of affairs will be such that their disability will never cause them suffering.

II Disability in primary Islamic sources
a) A Chapter (sūra) for the blind
The main Koranic documentation of celebrating the rights of the disabled and the blind in particular are the first verses (āyāt) of the Sura 80, Chapter A'mā:

> "The Prophet frowned and turned away.
> Because there came to him the blind man, [interrupting].
> But what would make you perceive, [O Muhammad], that perhaps he might be purified.
> Or be reminded and the remembrance would benefit him? As for he who thinks himself without need,
> To him you give attention. And not upon you [is any blame] if he will not be purified. But as for he who came to you striving [for knowledge] While he fears [Allah], From him you are distracted".
> (Sura 80, A'ma 1-10)

According to what is widely believed by exegetes to be the circumstance of the revelation of the above quoted verses, a number of the Quraysh tribe chiefs were in Prophet Muhammad's company and he was busy preaching Islam to them in the hope that his words would find an echo in their hearts. Meanwhile, 'Abd Allāh ibn Maktūm, a blind and indigent man, joined the meeting, and asked the prophet to recite and teach him some Koranic verses. Repeating his request and not staying still, he so much interrupted the prophet that the he got upset, an expression of discontentment crossing his face, thinking to himself: "these Arab chiefs will say among themselves that Muhammad's followers are the blind and slaves". Hence, he turned away from 'Abd Allāh and went on to talk with the group. At this moment, the above quoted verses were sent down, and the prophet was reproached. Afterwards, 'Abd Allāh ibn Maktūm was always honored by the prophet, and whenever he saw 'Abd Allh, he said: "greetings to the man because of whom I was reproached by my God", and went on to ask him "do you need me to do anything for you?"

The Koranic evidence can be regarded as a propitious turning point in the critique of the Islamic traditional theology as regards the disabled. The Chapter A'mā does not pursue hero-nurturing, saint-building, objectification of the disabled, and denial of their agency and free will, but seeks to recognize disability and confer identity on the disabled individual as a common believer and follower of the prophet. These verses can be well exploited to reconstruct the Islamic view of disability.

b) Prophets and Imams with Disability

The other cited evidence for honoring the disabled consists in a number of Koranic verses and Shiite Imams' hadiths depicting some prophets as disabled, emphasizing that their disability did not preclude their sacredness and mission. Shu'ayb, Job, Jacob, and Isaac are among such prophets. In the life stories of Shiite Imams too, there are apparent cases of disability: the disability of the daughter of the Prophet, Fāṭimat al-Zahrā ending in her demise; the disability of Abu-l-Faḍl al-'Abbās (the brother of the third Shiite Imam, Ḥusayn) who was the great commander of the Battle of Karbala and is always titled as the paragon of the disabled and the date of whose birth is called in Iran the day of "life-sacrificer" (*jānbāz*) in memory of all the war-wounded and the war-maimed; the severe disease and disability of the fourth Shiite Imam, 'Alī ibn al-Ḥusayn during the Battle of Karbala, which prevented him from taking part in the battle but never contaminated his sacredness and infallibility as an "Imam"; as well as the severe diseases of all the 11 Shiite Imams in their last days. According to the Shi'a, all the Imams except for the Promised Imam were martyred through assassination, but their infallibility and Imamate were never impugned in days of disease and disability or in their last days.

c) Charter of Mālik al-Ashtar

The letter from Imam 'Alī to Mālik al-Ashtar, also known as Charter of Mālik al-Ashtar, is another significant historical document emphasized by the disabled's rights campaigns. Mālik al-Ashtar was appointed by Imam 'Alī to govern Egypt, and the charter includes Imam 'Alī's recommendations to him and other governors. The following is the part concerning the rights of the disabled: "I warn you about a community impoverished by the hardships of the time, about those who have no way of earning a living, including the homeless and needy and people lacking in motor or mental powers. Allocate part of the public treasury to them; allocate part of the grains from the government-owned and Muslims' booty lands throughout the Islamic world. Discrimination is prohibited. Treat them as equal, for the most distant of them are like the closest of them. Observe the rights of all the needy. Welfare and enjoyment should not cause neglect about them. Do not let their rights be spoiled under the pretext of important and numerous jobs. Do not withhold your efforts from them. Do not show off to them, and do not turn away from them out of arrogance. Be modest because of God so that God makes you ascend. (*al-Hayat*, vol. 6, p.657)."

The historical document is very appropriate when it comes to looking after the disabled and avoiding tyranny and injustice against them. However, although in many parts of the charter, a great deal of attention has been paid to the dignity of, and respect for, the disabled, and such attention is very felicitous, the document does not tell us much about conferring an independent identity on disability as a diversified human experience and a physical and mental style.

III Disability in the life and teaching (al-sīra) of the Holy Prophet's and the Imams

Broadly speaking, the focus of hadiths from the Holy Prophet and Imams is on the following subjects.

a) Helping the disabled and giving alms to them

> The Holy Prophet said: "The gold in the world cannot be used to put a price on a minuscule part of the deed of he who walks a blind person

forty steps. And if he stops a blind person from falling down into a pit, the reward for his deed is higher than 100000 times of giving alms, and such good deeds override all their sins, obliterate them and make him ascend to the Higher Paradise." (*Bihar al-Anwar*, vol. 72, p. 15)

The Holy Prophet said: "He who satisfies the needs of a blind person, God bestows upon him both security from hell and security from hypocrisy, satisfies 70000 of his needs and blesses him" (*Wasa'il al-Shi'a*, vol. 11. P. 565).

In these hadiths, rather than a call for the empowerment and a structural reform of the society which result in the disabled gaining their independence, it is the giving of alms which is repeatedly encouraged.

b) Modesty towards the disabled

The Fourth Shiite Imam, 'Alī ibn al-Ḥusayn, passed by and greeted a few lepers who were eating. Yet he returned to them, saying "God does not like the arrogant. Now I am fasting, but you come over to my house. They did, and he lavished them with food and such (*Bihar al-Anwar*, vol. 72 p. 15)"

The Sixth Shiite Imam, Ja'far al-Ṣādiq said "Do not stare at the needy and disabled, as it is a sorrow to them" (*Bihar al-Anwar*, vol. 72 p. 15).

As a criticism of these hadiths, it could be said that basically if we consider people with disability as "the others", not "us", then there is a need to call for modesty towards them: after all, we do not call for us to be humble toward us. Therefore, it is clear that this type of hadiths do not have a right understanding and perception of the category of disability.

c) "Blind-heartedness" and lack of knowledge of God as the "real blindness"

The Holy Prophet said: "the blind is not he whose eyes do not see, but he who lacks insights." (*Nahj al-Fasaha*, p. 455).

The Holy Prophet said: "good speech is measured not by abundance of talk but by contemplation and saying what is liked by God and his Messenger, and stammer is measured not by speaking but by the lack of knowledge about God." (*Nahj al-Fasaha* p. 503)

The problem with this kind of hadiths is that they do not recognize the identity of the blind as it is, and call for a change of the definition of blindness from visual impairment to blind-heartedness, and definition of stammer from inability to speak properly to lack of knowledge about God, as this is the only way they can make people accept the blind.

d) *Destiny of and patience with disability*
The Holy Prophet said: everything is predestined even disability and intelligence (*Nahj al-Fasaha*, p. 455).

The Holy Prophet said: ""God says "If I direct a calamity at a servant among my servants with respect to their body, property, and children, and yet they keep patient I will be too bashful to review his or her deeds in the Day of Judgment."" (*Nahj al-Fasaha*, p. 513).

""A blind man came up to the Messenger of God and requested: "Ask God to return my sight to me." "Is the Heaven more desirable to you or the return of your vision?" replied the Messenger of God. "Is Paradise the reward?" "God is too gracious to make his pious servant turn blind and then not to reward him with the Heaven.""

The problem with these hadiths is that they see something repulsive and ugly in the being of the disabled individual, which necessitates recommendation to them of patience and consolation of them with the reward. But why should the disabled individual suffer and then be patient at all, when there is the possibility that they conduct all of their desired activities without being characterized as flawed and defective?

e) *Assignments proportionate to the disabled's capabilities*
The Fifth Shiite Imam Muḥammad Bāqir said: "in the Day of Judgment, God reprehends his servants in proportion to the wisdom he had conferred upon them". (*Usul al-Kafi*, vol. 1, p. 36).

The eighth Shiite Imam 'Alī ibn Mūsā al-Riḍā said: "fast is not mandatory for an old person or a disabled youth who cannot fast because of extreme thirst and hunger or a pregnant woman for whom it is harmful to fast, and in return for each day they should give about 750 grams of food to the poor" (*Mustadrak al-Wasa'il*, vol. 1. 568).

The great deal of attention paid in the hadiths to how the disabled should do their jurisprudential tasks and leniency upon them are not problematic *per se*. But desired is more attention to the rights of the disabled than to their duties.

f) Warn not to have sexual relations with people with disability

The First Shiite Imam 'Alī ibn Abī Ṭālib said: "Do not marry the mentally disabled girls and women, as their companionship is blight and their children will be disabled and spoiled also" (*Wasa'il al-Shi'a*, vol. 14, p. 56).

The Sixth Shiite Imam Ja'far al-Ṣādiq said: "do you see deformed and ugly people? Their fathers had coitus with their wives when the latter had a period" (*Mahajjat al-Bayda'*, vol. 3, p. 113).

The Holy Prophet said: "'Ali! Do not have coitus with your wife at the beginning, in the middle, and at the end of the month, as she and the child will develop madness, leprosy, and disability (*Man La-Yahduruh al*-Faqih, vol. 3, p. 552)

The Messenger of God told Imam 'Alī ibn Abi Ṭālib: "'Ali! No one should talk while having coitus, as the child might be born dumb" (*Wasa'il al-Shi'a*, p. 87).

In those hadiths, we encounter blatant infringement of the rights of the disabled: the hadiths which through causing fear of the formation of an abnormal germ forbid certain things at the time of coitus. Such hadiths are just messages of humiliation of and insult to disabled individuals. Specifically, the hadith which even proscribes getting married with a mentally disabled woman clearly needs to be corrected and reconsidered in modern times, or else in it alone are shattered all our ideals of modernity at once: women's rights, the disabled's rights, and the disabled women's rights to get married, disabled women's rights to give birth to children, and abnormal foetus's rights.

IV Disability in Islamic Sciences; Islamic Jurisprudence on Disability

Later Islamic jurisprudence (*fiqh*) is the only Islamic science which deals with the issue of disability in detail. In late Jurisprudential texts, unprecedented discussions have been opened up: the jurisprudence of the hearing-impaired, the visually impaired, and the mentally disabled. These discussions of the disabled indicate that lately the status of the disabled has assumed importance. That is, however, not to say that it is a positive status. Relative to the Koranic evidence and the Charter of Mālik al-Ashtar, Islamic jurisprudence does not show much affection for the disabled. To fuqaha of the old era, the disabled were not an issue at all, as if they were not responsible (*mukallaf*) to do anything so that fuqaha need not say anything about their practice of the religion. In late Islamic jurisprudence which considers the issue of the disabled, only the duties of the disabled are addressed: the jurisprudential decrees on the motor-disabled, the mentally disabled, and the visually-impaired are discussed in detail, as though the disabled individual is not the source of duties on the others' shoulders and does not have any rights specific to them.

In Islamic jurisprudence, it does not end with the inadequate affection and merely putting assignment on the shoulders of the disabled: at times, it is driven into violence and ableism. Imams of congregational prayers are said to need to be in completely good health and have no bodily or mental defect which would repulse people. The Islamic seminary too refuses to admit individuals with the slightest degree of disability, including poor vision or stammer. The disabled's acceptance for Islamic seminary is absolutely forbidden! The High Council of the Islamic Seminary introduced in 1993 a motion according to which the acceptance for individuals into the Islamic seminary is conditional upon the ascertainment of complete health. And in 1995 in an administrative law, the management of the Islamic seminary interpreted health as "the applicant must not be mad and not have any physical disability", as if it is easier for Islamic seminary and religious congregations to turn the disabled away from themselves so as to prevent the religion from repulsing people. The arduous task of building a culture of accepting the diversity and plurality of the physical and mental styles is abandoned and Islamic seminary chooses the easy option of denial and exclusion of the disabled.

In the constitution of the Islamic Republic of Iran, the legal status of the disabled is a bit more satisfactory. For example, the disabled enjoy the right to stand as candidates in election campaigns and to become members of the parliament, ministers, or presidents.

V Disability in Islamic culture and civilization: introduction of the Muslim disabled literati and scientists

Another measure taken in our times to reform the religious culture of disability is the identification of disabled scholars, scientists, poets, and literati in the history of the Islamic civilization and culture in great Persia. The measures are taken to empower the disabled and build self-confidence in them for work and activities.

VI Disability in Islamic government: Ayatollah Khomeini and institutionalization for the people with disability

After the Islamic revolution of Iran in 1979, Ayatollah Khomeini's policy of institutionalization was striking. The sentence quoted from the Ayatollah is always written at the entrance of Iranian institutions operating in the area of disability: "Serving the disabled equals serving the Holy Prophet". Unprecedented in previous Iranian governments, the institutionalization was a great influence Ayatollah Khomeini had on handling the affairs of the disabled. One example of the institutionalization is the Aba Basir Center, an *Education Center for the Visually Impaired*. Another institutionalized cultural measures is the centralization of the Koranic education and activities of the disabled. However, it is noticeable that the institutions focus more on raising fund for the disabled, rather than building identity, empowerment and creating jobs.

References

Amos, Yong. 2007. *Theology and Down Syndrome, Reimaging Disability in Late Modernity*. Baylor University Press.
Selected Islamic References (in Farsi):
Hadi Gushayish, 'Abdullah. 2018. *Ara-yi Tafsiri-yi Shi'a darbari-yi Suri-yi A'ma; Mustanadat-i Huquq-i Fardi va Ijtima'i-yi Ma'lulan* (Shiite Interpretive Ideas of the Chapter A'ma, Documentation of the Rights of the Disabled). Tavanmandan Publications. [in Farsi]
Iffati, Qudratullah. 2011. *Suri-yi Rowshandilan; Takrim-i Nabinayan dar Quran-i Karim* [A Koranic Chapter for The Blind; Honoring The Blind in Koran]. Disability Cultural Center. [in Farsi]
Muhibburrahman, Muhammad Mahdi. 2017. *Namaz-i Ma'lulan bar asas-i Fiqh-i Shi'i* [The Prayers of The Disabled According to The Shiite Jurisprudence]. Tavanmandan Publications.
Nasr Isfahani, Abazar. 2019. *Rahnama-yi Manabi'-i Fiqhi va Huquqi, Ma'khazshinasi va Chikidi-yi Asar darbari-yi Ma'luliyyat-ha va Ma'lulan* [A Guide to The Jurisprudential and Legal Sources: Bibliography and Abstracts of Works on Disabilities and the Disabled]. Tavanmandan Publications. [in Farsi]
Nuri, 'Ali. 2015. *Huquq-i Ma'lulan-i Iran* [The Rights of Iran's Disabled People]. Disability Cultural Center. [in Farsi]
Nuri, 'Ali. 2020. Mabani-yi Huquq-i Ma'lulan: Idalat va Musavat (*Foundations of The Disabled's Rights: Justice and Equality*). Tavanmandan Publications. [in Farsi]
Nuri, Muhammad. 2016. *Fa'aliat-ha-yi Qur'ani-yi Jami'i-yi Ma'lulan* [The Koranic Activities of The Disabled's Society]. Disability Cultural Center. [in Farsi]
Nuri, Muhammad. 2018. *Huquq-i Ma'lulan bar asas-i Tafsir-i Ustad Muhammad Taqi Shari'ati* [The Disabled's Rights Based on The Interpretation of Professor Muhammad Taqi Shari'ati]. Tavanmandan Publications. [in Farsi]
Qasimi, A'zam. 2017. *Ahkam-i Shar'i-yi Ma'lulin-i Harikati bar asas-i Aray-i Ayatollah Sayyid Ali Husayni Sistani* [The Jurisprudential Decrees on the Motor-disabled according to Ayatollah Sayyid Ali Husayni Sistani]. Disability Cultural Center. [in Farsi]
Qasimi, A'zam. 2017. *Ahkam-i Shar'i-yi Ma'lulin-i Zihni bar asas-i Aray-i Ayatollah Sayyid Ali Husayni Sistani* [The Jurisprudential Decrees on The Mentally Disabled according to Ayatollah Sayyid Ali Husayni Sistani]. Disability Cultural Center. [in Farsi]
Qasimi, A'zam. 2017. *Ahkam-i Shar'i-yi Nabinayan bar asas-i Aray-i Ayatollah Sayyid Ali HusayniSistani* [The Jurisprudential Decrees on The Visually Impaired according to Ayatollah Sayyid Ali Husayni Sistani]. Disability Cultural Center. [in Farsi]

Disability and Perfection

BERNHARD NITSCHE

The article attempts to define the characteristics of disabled living as life in and with specific limitations. Disabled living displays in a particular way the finitude and limits of life and makes us aware of them. In view of limited life chances, the perfection of disabled life is marked in a special way by what Christian faith ultimately hopes for all life: flesh and blood are not raised, but all the vicissitudes and events that mark life are personalised, put right and perfected in preparation for a life of fullness.

I Life with disabilities
Anyone who approaches the topic of disability and perfection from an inclusive intellectual perspective will first have to realise that there can be an extremely wide range of human disabilities, affecting physical, mental, psychological and/or social functions. Of course, physical disability is the most visible. If a person lacks arms or legs, or because of paralysis can no longer move on their own and has to rely on a wheelchair, we can immediately see that they are disabled. The diagnosis is more difficult in the case of people with slight to moderate limitations of their cognitive or mental faculties. Recurrent depression or permanent learning difficulties and limitations in coping cognitively with tasks or life events are possible examples. In the current debate we should also not forget the victims of sexual abuse or other forms of violence – including and especially in Church contexts. Finally, many people have multiple disabilities that aggravate aspects of physical, psychological, intellectual and social limitations.

Generally disabled people display limitations of human life particularly seriously in specific areas. Disability can be linked to difficult turning-points in one's life and severe limitations in carrying on with one's life. What does a manual worker do if their arms and fingers are suddenly paralysed? How does a wheelchair user organise her life if she can only sit for periods of two to three hours? How does a person with cognitive and psychological limitations pursue their activity if they easily get stressed or intermittently cannot concentrate? As someone affected by disability myself, I think it is important not to deny this reality of specific limitations and restrictions. They mean that inclusion also requires measures that support integration. Of course disabilities are also 'created'; how they are dealt with in practice is socially determined. In this connection I realise that the way disabled people process their experience differs between people who have acquired a disability and people who have grown up with their disability from birth and feel that their existence is a healthy 'normality'. Disabilities can also make other people aware that their own lives – in contrast to the mechanisms for making life move faster and constantly increasing performance – is a life surrounded by limitations. In contrast to the pressure for higher, faster, further that comes from permanent optimisation and maximalisation, people with specific limitations can remind all other people that our lives are lives with finite resources and limited possibilities, and yet can be good and happy lives.

II My own life can be good

The essential goodness of one's own life can be experienced and internalised when it is cultivated in a network of parental and social relationships, when fundamental affirmation, appreciation for one as a person and approval of what one does are given symbolic expression. Ideally, family and friends or particular groups and communities are the places where diverse individuals find understanding, respectful and positive support. This allows people to develop creatively and, at best, work to create the conditions for a successful and happy life. This requires encouragement from others, incentives within the community and targeted development of an individual's talents. Naturally developing one's own potential requires (high) intrinsic motivation and effort on the individual's part. It requires expert training and personal development, education and help. The development of an individual's potential is presumably all the greater the more it is shared by a group of identifiable people in the same situation, and constructed reciprocally. Rather than an 'objectifying' functional view that subjects people to external performance criteria and permanent testing, and makes them the objects of outside expectations and evaluations designed to meet the demands of a system or to instrumentalise them for predefined interests and measures, as a rule people develop in a free environment of trusting goodwill. In this way, despite handicaps, people can begin to feel valuable and significant. A person who grows up in such an encouraging social environment and is able to shape their life amidst trusting goodwill can contribute their own wishes and ideas, will discover their own creativity with greater freedom and self-confidence, will develop their talents more courageously and energetically, and will more resolutely develop a productive resistance to the pressure imposed by the burden of life in and with disability. Similarly, disabled people, if they have accepted their situation, and shaped their disabled life positively, can in some circumstances reach a position in which they can look in a more relaxed way at their own finitude and nakedness (Gen 3.7, 10). Sometimes disabilities can even be a launch-pad for specific chances and potential. For example, it is not impossible for a person who is blind to develop their hearing and musical skill to a remarkable extent, or they may have particularly developed their concentration and learning capacity as a result of the limitation on the information flow they are exposed to. People with Down syndrome can develop high emotional competence and social sensitivity. People who are physically disabled can produce first-rate cognitive and professional achievements and even win titles in competitive sport at the Paralympics. These things become possible when internal motivation is extremely strong and – metaphorically speaking – outward invalidity does not become inner invalidity.

III Biblical anthropology – the whole person

The bible is always concerned with the whole person. The biblical terms used to describe human life indicate the finite existence of human beings, which can only be understood in relation to God and as derived from God. It would be wrong to see this as competing with the possibilities and power that come from God. The perspective of human life as a result of God's support is shaped especially by the promise of royal dignity resulting from being created in God's image (Gen 1.27-28). The human being's dignity is defined by the autonomy made possible by freedom and through his relationship to his or her self, to other human beings and through a sovereign concern for creation as the house of life. This dignity becomes visible in the capacity for self-transcendence and through the development of other possibilities of shaping life. In the light of the image of God they embody, human freedom, human accomplishments and the momentary bodiliness of human beings are an existence unlocked by God and a gift of grace. Human existence is thus filled and fulfilled in these various dimensions of human existence. As an underlying melody, the bible stresses that the source of human beings does not lie within themselves. A human being is taken from stardust and brought to life by the inbreathing of God's breath and inspired by God's spiritual nature (Gen 2.7). Various levels thus belong together: the vital inward-directed level in bodiliness, the personal level expressed in activity and personality, the social level of relationships to the world around us, and the transcendental level of free thought and free action implied in subjectivity. A human being can understand the process of increasing this potential as life. If this is so, a full life would be the greatest self-intimacy and intimacy with others and the maximum expansion of inherent possibilities. This also applies when they emerge from shock, disillusion or the reductive effect of hereditary or acquired disability.

On the other hand, diminishment or injury may in extreme cases be combined with relationship death (loss of a partner, loss of contact and activity), professional death (unfitness to work, inability to earn a living), or with a gradual physical death (acute multiple sclerosis). To the extent that disability is also associated with severely reduced life expectancy and amputated life prospects, creation, intended as good, can be experienced as life in suffering, futility, loneliness and sadness, and this awakens, possibly with rage, a cry for justice and fullness and the penetrating question of theodicy.

If disability involves a situation in which human life is drastically limited, the vision of perfection in the end-time, in heaven, has to insist that even a disabled life is a genuine human life. This means that everything that is said about the perfection of human nature in God and through God applies also to disabled people. The limitations and difficult living conditions must not be exaggerated, even though they have had a deep impact on the life and career of a disabled person and the development of their personality. Perfection – as with the marks of Christ's wounds – cannot be thought of apart from these barriers and limitations, but only as achieved through them. This means, however, that there is always an abundance of chances and potential that have remained undiscovered and uncultivated, which have only been seen in rudimentary form and could only receive completely satisfactory development in an individual life in fortunate cases. It is only life in and with the specific limits of disability that shows that there are things that remain uncompensated and unredeemed. This increases the level of conflict with the divine promise for the future of creation according to which every life has been ordained by God for good possibilities that will come to perfection in the sabbath of the end-time in which God's power has full scope (Gen 1.31).

IV Philosophical phenomenology: the concept of the body

The German language and philosophical phenomenology distinguish between two words for 'body', *Körper* and *Leib*. The *Leib*, as part of a human being's intentional relationship to the world, is the medium of being-in-the-world, which feels and is felt from within. In it and through it sensations are subjectively grasped as sensations.[1] According to Maurice Merleau-Ponty, the *Leib* is not an object, but 'the vehicle of being-towards-the-world', pure openness to the world. Accordingly, the *Leib* is 'always beside me and constantly there for me'.[2] In contrast, the *Körper* denotes the objectivity of chemical and physical elements and biological structures of human nature that is subsequently grasped, examined and abstracted. Whereas the physical *Körper* and its biological structures are visible to the senses and can be physically measured, the *Leib* that belongs to me unlocks a prior and immediate field of presence, which can be felt.

In English, the distinction might be expressed as one between an external and internal perspective, between the *material-natural-objective body* and the *intentional-spiritual-subjective body*. The first denotes the chemical and physical materiality of the cells and biological structures of the body, the second the form of expression of an intentional person towards the world that pervades the biological and material dimension.[3]

We see therefore that the concept of the *Leib* leads us to distinguish between different levels of human existence: first, *personhood*, which is defined by the first-person perspective. Then there is the world of objects, which we see as physical bodies (*Körper*) constituted in time and space. Third, there is the level of the *Leib*, which performs a mediating function between bodiliness and personality and manifests the intentional process of a human being's relationship to society and the world in their bodiliness.

V Resurrection and transformation in death

This distinction allows us to say the following about human eschatology.[4] In addition to their link to the world and society mediated by their bodies, human beings are significantly determined by a self-understanding. This enables a person to become aware of himself or herself and to interiorise the impacts and impressions left by their life. This gives rise to a personal self-image, which is constantly re-formed. Through the 'I'-consciousness of the first-person perspective human beings become aware of their links to themselves, society and the world, become active in them in a personal way. To be able to speak of the personhood of a human being requires the lasting, numerical identity of the Ego. This is the source of the person's continuity in their identity, which is constructed in the flux of events and histories. Thus the transition from mortal to immortal life, from earthly to supernatural existence, and from worldly time to the transcendent time of God, is on the one hand God's doing. It is God who brings about the lasting and transformative empowerment of human beings. On the other hand, this transition is the human being's own doing. From our earthly perspective this transition can only be imagined and expressed in temporal categories. To this extent a human being's last act in their dying surrender to death is the other side of the first act of their entry into the supernatural reality of God. Because in the infinity and eternity of God there are no longer any spatial or temporal structures, what escapes our necessarily spatio-temporally constructed imagination merges into the non-time and non-space of God. Interiorisation and intensification take place in the personalisation of biographical identity. Through this process the life-experience of bodily, mental, psychological or social disability is preserved when the biological structures collapse and the body's matter decays, to become part of the matter of the cosmos and its increasing entropy.

This personalisation can ensure that the unimagined entry into the totally other reality of God transcends the inadequate concept of a zombie eschatology. This envisages, if not the revival of the corpse, a post-death reassembly of the biochemical matter and the reconstitution of the earthly body. But the transformation that takes place in death is something different from the biological or genetic transformation of a caterpillar in this physical world into a beautiful butterfly within this physical world or the reconstitution of the former body through an absurd collecting together of the material components that have been scattered far and wide and already become part of other entities. Resurrection takes place in death, not afterwards. It is not some not some post-death action on a corruptible or already corrupt corpse.[5]

Resurrection and perfection in death means that a person, with all their successful and failed relationships, with all their developed or undeveloped gifts and talents, with all the redeemed and unredeemed elements of their personality, with their happiness and sufferings, with their pains and disease, with their successes and failures, with their mortality and fullness of life, in other words, with the whole of their successful and unsuccessful life, enters the reality of God transfigured, that is, purified, put right and made eternal in fullness. In this way human beings receive as a gift a share in the immortality of the One who alone has immortality (1 Tim 6.16). In this life and immortality saved in and through death there takes place the radical transformation of the human person's unique, particular history in its body-soul totality. When God comes at the end and meets a person, especially a disabled person, the finitude of earthly life is transformed into the superabundance of heavenly life: 'In the process the earlier failed, destroyed, rejected relationships and the person's unattained possibilities are not merely recognised, rather they are transformed, made whole, set right by purification, redeemed in a fulfilling perfection that is a new identity for eternal life.'[6]

VI The biblical message of transformation

According to one saying of Jesus, this new way of being in God and with God is like that of 'angels in heaven' (Mk 12.24-27). And Paul, in the perspective of his expectation of God's imminent coming, emphasises: 'So it is with the resurrection of the dead. What is sown is perishable, what is raised is imperishable. It is sown in dishonour, it is raised in glory.

It is sown in weakness, it is raised in power... Just as we have borne the image of the man of dust, we will also bear the image of the man of heaven (1 Cor 15.42-44, 49). Paul rejects any idea of the revival of the earthly (disabled) body or its reconstitution when he goes on: 'Flesh and blood cannot inherit the kingdom of God, nor does the perishable inherit the imperishable.... we will all be changed (1 Cor 50-51).

When God comes to meet a person at death, that person's life and their self are transformed into a glory that transcends human imagination: "What no eye has seen, nor ear heard, nor the human heart conceived, what God has prepared for those who love him' (1 Cor 2.9). If it is true of people on earth, and perhaps especially for disabled people, that they are not yet what they could be and would really like to be, that means that they are searching for their true, full identity, the identity that they can live in relation to themselves, to other people, to their history and the world to which they belong in complete happiness and reconciliation. Genes, socialisation, relationships and achievement, what has occurred through one's own or others' fault, perfection transcends all this. The process of transformation means cleansing, transformation and the fulfilment of the person defined in their continuity before and after death, with all their relationships and longings, in preparation for an identity unlocked, intended and even deeply longed for by God. Inclusion into the full life of the community of the resurrected is at once superabundance of possibilities and overflowing joy at communion with God and the heavenly rediscovery of other creatures. In such a heavenly community of mutual inspiration and reciprocal enjoyment, everything is brought to perfection in the liberated and liberating dance in the glory of God. Death is monotonous, but not God's new creation in the new heaven and on the new earth (Rev 21.1), with 'the powers of the age to come' (Heb 6.5), so that 'everyone freely receives his or her due and all together enjoy the fullness of eternal life'.[7] This includes the adoption of Christ's existence into oneself, and as part of this the transfigured marks of Christ's wounds. Just as they become transparent as signs of God's unconditional love, faithfulness and sacrifice, so the wounds of disability become intelligible as signs of true human existence both for one's own life and for the lives of others. That very life, filled with pain, racked by suffering, that fell short, and all that never came to fruition, is shaped into the image of the heavenly One: 'And all of us, with unveiled faces, seeing the glory of the Lord as though reflected in a mirror, are being transformed into the same image from one degree of glory to another; for this comes from the Lord, the Spirit' (2 Cor 3.18). And where the outer person is ground down and destroyed, 'our inner nature is being renewed day by day' (2 Cor 4.16). Logically what is being described is a process in which a person is transformed into his or her true self, entirely imbued with Christ. In the Christian vision that is already a task for this life. It is completed in the eternal existence, in the invisible world of God's infinity and immortality.

And so at the end we are left with the hope that all the complaints and tears, all the obstacles and disappointments, all the pains and suffering of all human beings and all creatures will not only find their consolation in the One who will wipe every tear away (Rev 21.4). There is still another hope, that all the meaninglessness and all our failures to understand, all the incomprehensibility of suffering, every cry of despair, will find an answer full of love that human beings are unable to give. An answer from the One who loves all things that exist (Wis 11.24) and has promised life in abundance (Jn 10.10).

Translated by Francis McDonagh

Notes

1. Edmund Husserl, *Husserliana, Band IV: Ideen zu einer reinen Phänomenologie und Phänomenologischen Philosophie*, ed. Marly Biemel, Tübingen, 1952, p. 151.
2. Maurice Merleau-Ponty, *Phänomenologie der Wahrnehmung, aus dem Französischen übersetzt und eingeführt durch eine Vorrede von Rudolf Böhm*, Berlin, 1966, pp 106, 115. English translation: *Phenomenology of Perception*, trans. Donald Landes, London, 2012.
3. On this, see also Thomas Schärtl, 'Was heißt "Auferstehung des Leibes"?', in Godehard Brüntrup, Matthias Rugel and Maria Schwartz (ed.), *Auferstehung des Leibes – Unsterblichkeit der Seele?*, Stuttgart, 2010, pp 59-80.
4. On this, see Hans Kessler, 'Personale Identität und leibliche Auferstehung? Systematisch-theologische Überlegungen. Response auf Georg Gasser', in Georg Gasser, Ludwig Jaskolla and Thomas Schärtl (ed.), *Handbuch für analytische Theologie*, Münster 2017, pp 641-666. Cf Josef Wohlmuth, *Mysterium der Verwandlung. Eine Eschatologie aus katholischer Perspektive im Gespräch mit jüdischem Denken der Gegenwart* (*Studien zu Judentum und Christentum*), Paderborn 2005.
5. On the discussion of the concept of resurrection in death, see Oscar Cullman, 'Unsterblichkeit der Seele oder Auferstehung der Toten? Die Antwort des Neuen

Testamentes', in Godehard Brüntrup, Matthias Rugel and Maria Schwartz (ed.), *Auferstehung des Leibes – Unsterblichkeit der Seele?, Stuttgart, 2010, pp 13-24 (English ed. Immortality of the Soul or Resurrection of the Dead? The witness of the New Testament,* London, 1958); Matthias Reményi, *Um der Hoffnung willen. Untersuchungen zur eschatologischen Theologie Jürgen Moltmanns,* Regensburg, 2005, pp 181-285, esp. 212-242.
6. Hans Kessler, 'Personale Identität und leibliche Auferstehung? Systematisch-theologische Überlegungen. Response auf Georg Gasser', p. 656.
7. Jürgen Moltmann, *Im Ende – der Anfang,* Gütersloh, 2003, p. 180 (English ed. *In the End-The Beginning. The life of Hope,* London and Minneapolis, MN, 2004; also available as an e-book: https://www.worldcat.org/title/in-the-end-the-beginning-the-life-of-hope/oclc/1132361619?referer=br&ht=edition

Part Four: Reforming the Church

History and Comments of EDAN at the WCC

SAMUEL GEORGE

An attempt is made in this article to map the history of the issue of disability in the ecumenical circles especially in the World Council of Churches. Various turning points/shifts in the WCC through EDAN are highlighted in this journey. A brief argument is made to present disability both as a theology and mission of the church and how EDAN has contributed and shaped it.

I Introduction
Disability was never seen "cool" even as a methodology for engaging with issues related to God-human-creation – the primary focus of theology. It took years if not decades to transcend from a medical model of disability to a social model of disability which, is very crucial for disability studies. It is in this light one needs to understand the importance of Ecumenical Disability Advocates Network (EDAN) a unit of the World Council of Churches (WCC).

II Brief History of EDAN
Since early 1970's the WCC has treated the issue of disability as an important concern of the Christian Church,[1] but the first great evidence was when the WCC fifth General Assembly in Nairobi (1975) issued a statement on „The Handicapped and the Wholeness of the Family of God." and the WCC's Sixth Assembly in Vancouver, Canada in 1983, invited 21 people with disabilities as part of the Assembly participants.

Further the "Theology of Life Study" drew on the experiences of local groups from around the world, to ground WCC's theology more firmly in the lived experiences of local communities around the globe including persons with disabilities brought about an interim statement on the „Theological and Sociological Understanding of the Issue of Disabilities" in 1997 which was prepared by a Working Group. With a new title of „Interim Statement on the Theological and Empirical Understanding of the Issue of Disabilities" it was sent to member churches, regional ecumenical organizations and national councils of churches. In the accompanying letter the WCC General Secretary, dr. Konrad Raiser, wrote: „This document presents what may be a new perspective for many churches: that congregations need the presence of people with disabilities. ‚The parts of the body which seem to be weaker are indispensable.' (1 Corinthians 12:22)."

EDAN was born during the 1998 WCC 8th Assembly in Harare, Zimbabwe, when 10 persons with disabilities, in their role as advisors, took the opportunity to deliberate how best to influence the churches to recognize and incorporate persons with disabilities in their witness and service program. It was through this consultation that the advisors decided to form the Ecumenical Disability Advocates Network (EDAN) as a vehicle that would carry WCC's work on disability by giving it a new form that would give it continuity and visibility in the churches. The headquarters were placed in Kenya and in December 1999 objectives and structures have been fixed.[2] The theological document – "A Church for All and of All" was a historical moment in the life of church and WCC. This document addresses and challenges the churches to be inclusive and holistic in its nature and practice.[3]

The document raised the challenge of ministerial formation from the perspective of disability. Since 2004 EDAN has partnered with the WCC Ecumenical Theological Education Desk and embarked on engaging theological institutions in disability discourse. This was done on two-levels. First, to engage with theological institutions to train and encourage them to develop curriculum on disability issues and producing theological materials from disability perspectives. Second, it also trained lay communities by organizing training programs for them.

Another important milestone in its influence was partnering with various national and regional councils. EDAN has also partnered with non-church institutions like the United Nations and various regional and federal government institutions.

During the restructuring that followed the WCC ninth General Assembly in 2006 at Porto Alegre, EDAN's work was placed within Programme 2 on Unity, Mission, Evangelism and Spirituality. This has provided an opportunity for it to benefit greatly from the WCC call to the churches for visible Unity in which, all gifts and contribution at individual level are indispensable for the building of one church of Christ.[4] The WCC tenth General Assembly in Busan in 2013 reaffirmed the works of EDAN as central to the mission and purpose of the WCC.

Disability, Theology and Mission of the Church

Theology is a public discipline (as such it seeks a universal language-meaning) but it is also a discipline that critically examines the languages and symbols of particular traditions and in our case the Christian tradition.[5] However, what is interesting here is theology both as a public discipline and as a particular Christian reflection have failed to address the issue of disability. The major reason being its obsession with ableism. Disability theology (or theology from a disability perspective) problematizes the traditional ableist tendencies in theology and begins with the shared experiences of the people with disability.

Notable also is the perceived absence of disability issues in the missional discussions. It is much more crucial in the context of the challenges presented by the world's largest minority (according to a rough estimate PWDs represent around 15% of world population) and they do not find mention in the mission discussions. The fundamental question raised by PWDs is – are they object of mission or they are equal partners in the *Missio Dei*.[6] Bevans writes, Mission precedes the church. Mission is first of all God's. God shares that mission with women and men. Mission calls the church into being to serve God's purpose in the world. The church does not have a mission, but the mission has a church.[7] So the question is: in that mission of God what is the role of PWDs?

Since its inception, EDAN has embarked on a **Mission** to "advocate for the inclusion, participation and active involvement of persons with disabilities in all spiritual, social, economic and structural life of the church and society" with a **Vision** of "Church of All and for All, an epitome of truly inclusive community."[8]

One major way EDAN has done it through prioritizing theological education as the area where disability issues will be fostered. In hindsight, one can say that to a great extent they have been successful in integrating the disability issues to the mainstream theological education. The objective here is aimed at influencing inclusion of persons with disabilities in these institutions both as students as well as faculty members but even more importantly, to prepare theological students for ministry with and among persons with disabilities as a way to improve the attitudes held by the churches and society on persons with disabilities. Today, through the efforts of EDAN-WCC disability issues are taught in several institutions around the globe. The works of EDAN are divided into various regions: the **Middle East** (Lebanon, Egypt, Jordan); **Caribbean** (Jamaica, Haiti, Barbados, Trinidad and Tobago, Cuba); **Asia** (India, Myanmar, Sri Lanka, Bangladesh, Taiwan, Indonesia, Philippines, Korea); **Latin America** (Bolivia, Mexico, Columbia, Argentina, Ecuador); **Europe**; **North America** (Association of Theological School, NCC of USA); **Pacific** (Solomon Islands, Tahiti, Samoa, Fiji, Tonga, Cook Island, Davuilevu); **Africa** (Kenya, Ghana, Congo, Uganda, Tanzania, Zimbabwe, Botswana, Malawi, South Africa, Burundi, Rwanda, Nigeria).

EDAN has been engaged in advocacy for inclusive community for all with the churches from its inception. The EDAN and ETE (Program on Ecumenical Theological Education) came to realize that without addressing the issue in theological colleges it will not make much impact in the life of the church and society. It was discussed that to institutionalize the issue, EDAN and ETE decided to launch a program on „Disability and Theological Discourse" in 2016. Samuel Kabue, the Program Executive of EDAN-WCC and Wati Longchar,[9] Consultant ETE initiated several consultations in Asia and Pacific.

Another very important contribution that EDAN-WCC has made is to develop theological-missiological materials for training future leaders of the church. WCC has published within the Risk Book Series. Also, *International Review of Mission*, *Ecumenical Review* and *EDAN Newsletter* have regularly published scholarly articles on disability theology. Many resource materials are now available through active partnership between EDAN and other like-minded institutions (ETE-CCA, ATESEA, BTESSC, PTC, SPATS, PERSETIA, ATEM, ATIEA).

Conclusion

It took a movement like EDAN-WCC to take up the challenge of addressing the important issue of disability from theological, missiological and ecclesiological perspective. And since its inception in 1998 it has created an important buzz in the Christian circles and its impacts are quite evident in the number of institutions teaching disability theology and publishing from the perspective of the PWDs.

Notes

1. Further informations could be found in http://www.wcc-coe.org/wcc/what/jpc/hist.html.
2. Cfr. https://www.oikoumene.org/en/resources/documents/wcc-programmes/unity-mission-evangelism-and-spirituality/just-and-inclusive-communities/people-with-disabilities/reports/first-global-meeting-kenya (accesed April 2020). Later there was the creation of reference groups for various regions.
3. See Arne Fritzon and Samuel Kabue, Interpreting Disability. A Church for All and of All, Geneve: WCC 2004.
4. See http://www.edan-wcc.org/index.php/about-us/history (accessed January 08, 2016).
5. Robert Cummings Neville, *A Theology* Primer (New York: State University of New York Press, 1991), xiv.
6. For a good discussion on Mission from Missiological perspective cf. Benjamin T. Conner, "Enabling Witness: Disability in Missiological Perspective," *Journal of Disability and Religion* 19, no. 1 (March 2015): 15-29.
7. Stephen B. Bevans and Roger P. Schroeder, *Prophetic Dialogue: Reflections on Christian Mission Today* (Maryknoll, New York: Orbis Books, 2011), 15-16.
8. http://www.edan-wcc.org/index.php/about-us/who-we-are (accessed January 08, 2016).
9. Dr. A. Wati Longchar in his role as the Consultant ETE and Director in-Charge of BTESSC/SATHRI has played a very crucial role in the introduction and furtherance of disability studies in the Indian theological context.

'Finding Something for Bénédicte to Do': What Place can Women with Learning Difficulties Have in the Eucharistic Liturgy?

TALITHA COOREMAN-GUITTIN

In the last few years Pope Francis has frequently appealed for people living with disabilities to be allowed to take their full place in the Church, especially in catechesis and liturgy. Nevertheless we are finding that it is not always easy to find an appropriate place suitable for everyone. The place of women with learning difficulties in the Eucharist has not really been given much thought. This article sets out to examine the possibility that a woman with learning difficulties could act as an acolyte in the Eucharistic liturgy.

I Introduction

Allow me to introduce you to Bénédicte, whose experience will be the basis for raising some theological and Church-related questions by comparing it with statements of official teaching. Experiences of faith, as elements of a living tradition that has still not finished and is still in the process of creation (*in statu viae*), reveal the paths by which the Word comes to meet women and men of today.[1] According to Étienne Grieu, describing these experiences allows us to discover 'the prodigious capacity of the God of Jesus Christ to set his extraordinary power to music in the most ordinary of existences'.[2]

Bénédicte has just retired, after years of ironing other people's clothes, cleaning other people's houses and serving other people's meals. Bénédicte has moderate learning difficulties. 'I like to be useful,' she tells me.'
For some years now Bénédicte has been in the habit of helping the parish priest to prepare the Eucharistic table. She saw correctly that there are no longer enough altar-servers to do this. So, at the offertory, she jumps up from her seat in the assembly and brings the bread and wine to the altar. The priest is very grateful for this spontaneity.
But there's been a change of parish priest and a new priest is celebrating in our parish. He is disoriented by Bénédicte's actions and won't have someone at the altar who's not wearing an alb. I suggest that Bénédicte be taught to be an altar-server and found an alb to fit her. The priest isn't keen. 'Of course we'll find something for Bénédicte to do,' he tells me. 'She can be useful in a different way.'

This incident saddens me. The priest's attitude shows that we still have some way to go for people with learning difficulties to be able to play their full part in the Church and more specifically during the liturgy. It's not just about 'finding something for Bénédicte to do' to make her feel useful. That's not the issue, at least not really. Bénédicte doesn't need occupational therapy. The issue is much more important than that.

The case of Bénédicte, which combines learning difficulties, age and being female, raises as a matter of urgency the question of the role of women with disabilities in the Church. The key question is: how can we see something of the unfathomable mystery of God who takes on our condition of human vulnerability, a condition also revealed in people with learning difficulties? How are we to recognise what God wants to tell us through them? Through the presence of this person, what line of thinking does the ecclesial community suggest to the faithful parishioners? In this article I explore the possible place of a woman with a learning difficulty as an acolyte in the Eucharistic liturgy. My reflection develops in three stages: a critical look at the Roman instruction *Redemptionis Sacramentum* from the perspective of disability, followed by a reflection on what it means to be priest, prophet and king for a person with a learning difficulty. The third section juxtaposes the idea of the common priesthood of the faithful with some words of Pope Francis's. Finally I offer some aesthetic considerations and develop the idea of the *via turpitudinis* as a path to faith.

II Applying the rules: the Instruction *Redemptionis Sacramentum*

Can we even deny Bénédicte the right to serve the Lord at His table? Our priest is very familiar with the authoritative Roman texts on the subject of the celebration of the Eucharist. Isn't he only applying the rules? It is in fact easy to deny Bénédicte access to the altar on the basis of a superficial reading of the Instruction *Redemptionis Sacramentum* because this text says:

> It is altogether laudable to maintain the noble custom by which boys or youths... provide service of the altar after the manner of acolytes, and receive catechesis regarding their function in accordance with their power of comprehension.[3]

Obviously, at 60, Bénédicte is neither a boy nor a young person – though the idea of 'young' could lead to a lengthy discussion. Bénédicte has the cognitive development of a 10-year old child....

Later on, the Instruction allows for the possibility (with restrictions) for girls *and* women to become altar-servers. This explicit mention of girls *and* women implies that adult women are meant. It is therefore difficult to exclude Bénédicte on the basis of this text purely because of her age. So is she excluded because of her disability ? There is no reference to learning difficulties in the Instruction, but it does open up an interesting perspective when it explicitly refers to 'capacities' (French) or 'powers of comprehension' (English). 'According to their capacities' can be understood as 'whatever their capacities'. Bénédicte's intellectual capacities are impaired, but that does not prevent her from receiving suitable training to become an acolyte. The text was not drafted with this in mind, but perhaps there is an opening here.

> However, the same paragraph of *Redemptionis Sacramentum* conditions the possibility of women becoming altar-servers on the permission of the local bishop:

Girls or women may also be admitted to this service of the altar, at the discretion of the diocesan Bishop and in observance of the established norms .

The Holy See's reluctance to accept women as altar-servers is well-known, and was also explicit in Paul VI's *motu proprio Ministeria quaedam* of 1972.[4] It has been discussed within the Church, although the practice is well-established throughout the world.[5] Since no episcopal order has been issued in the diocese of Strasbourg, Bénédicte can be removed from serving at the altar on that principle alone. In practice, however, the annual diocesan meeting of altar-servers brings boys and girls to the bishop's side. There is another reason that could form the basis of a decision to refuse Bénédicte access to the altar. *Redemptionis Sacramentum* stipulates clearly: 'No one should be selected whose designation could cause consternation for the faithful' (46). This recommendation was made in 1973 by the Congregation for the Discipline of the Sacraments as a criterion for appointing extraordinary ministers of the Eucharist. Its intention was to exclude people whose way of life was not 'worthy of this great office'.[6] Bénédicte's life is worthy and in accord with the moral precepts of the Catholic Church. However, the way she behaves at the altar may surprise the faithful. Is that a sufficient reason? In my opinion, there is nothing shocking about her presence; it is narrow-mindedness that is shocked by this person with a disability. In a society that keeps people with learning difficulties at a distance and segregates them, it is not surprising that some worshippers are unable to understand the value of Bénédicte's active participation in the service of the altar, deriving as it does from her baptismal vocation.

III Priest, prophet and king…

The truth is that, by virtue of his or her baptism, every Christian receives the dignity of priest, prophet and king. The Vatican II Constitution on the Church gives a very clear vision of these three responsibilities: every baptised person, and without mention of their intellectual abilities, shares in the *tria munera Christi*, liturgy, witness and service. That means that in his or her suprême rôle as a baptised person, every baptised person, independently of their capacities, is called to the service of God and human beings (LG 10-13). The Council spells this out:

Thus both by reason of the offering and through Holy Communion all take part in this liturgical service, not indeed, all in the same way but each in that way which is proper to himself (LG 11).

Bénédicte certainly takes part in a way 'that is proper to herself' in the celebration of the liturgy. It is true that this paragraph of *Lumen Gentium* was not drafted specifically to allow people with learning difficulties to serve at the altar, but there is nothing to stop us reading it in that way. The presence of people with a disability at the altar has not yet come to the notice of the magisterium. There are no instructions approving of or forbidding such a presence. Nonetheless, in the diocese of Poitiers in 2013, for example, the conclusions of the synod expressly stipulated:

The service of the altar may be entrusted in the diocese to people with learning difficulties. The liturgical setting in which this service is performed will show the face of a Church that is fragile, resplendent and full of hope, the face of a Church that is welcoming and generous.[7]

In the view of the diocese of Poitiers, for people like Bénédicte to take part in the service of the altar is not simply 'symbolic', or an act of do-gooding; it is a sign of the power of God at the heart of vulnerability, of a life that is fruitful beyond appearances.[8]

This decision of the diocese of Poitiers in 2003 finds an echo in the words of Pope Francis, who defends the place of people with disabilities in society and *a fortiori* in the Church. Every person – independently of his or her abilities – is necessary to the body of Christ. *O tutti o nessuno*', 'everyone or no-one', Pope Francis had said on 11 June 2016 at a meeting with people with disabilities in the Vatican. Francis said in substance that if a priest didn't make everyone welcome, Francis would advise him to close the door of his church.[9] In 2017 he encouraged people with disabilities to make their authentic contribution to the life of the Church through their witness, in order to pass on the faith more effectively. The Pope was talking about access to the sacraments, but it's a safe bet that he wouldn't bat an eyelid about extending his logic to serving at the altar. He wrote:

Much progress has been made in the pastoral care of the disabled;

it is important to go forward, for example, better recognizing their apostolic and missionary capacity, and even before that, the value of their "presence" as people, as active members of the ecclesial Body. Hidden in weakness and frailty are treasures capable of renewing our Christian communities.

In welcoming Bénédicte's vulnerable presence at the heart of the Eucharist mystery, the Church would be showing that 'the members of the body that seem to be weaker are indispensable' (1 Cor 12.22). But the priest in our parish doesn't see it like that, so we had to deal with Bénédicte's situation.

When I explained to Bénédicte that she could no longer be an altar server, she didn't seem sad. She's used to being disappointed. She just said, seriously: 'I understand.' I tried to smile. Full inclusion, mutual respect – for the moment that's our heavenly Jerusalem.
Two weeks later she came up to me at the end of mass. 'I'd like to read at mass,' she said. I said 'OK,' and then I realised – Bénédicte can't read. But that doesn't matter; she has an excellent memory. She'll be able to learn the reading by heart. Over two weeks we slowly learn the reading from the book of Deuteronomy. When the great day of her reading arrives, Bénédicte, all smiles, comes with me to the altar. She looks at the assembly confidently. She knows the text ; she doesn't have to read. In her slow, halting voice she declaims: 'Moses said to his people: the Lord will send you a prophet like me.'
I look at Bénédicte in amazement. The prophetic force of this text had passed me by until now.

Yes, that day Bénédicte was a prophet for us, even if not all the people present understood it like that. Some were too surprised to see this 'retarded' woman at the lectern to be able to listen to her. Others didn't even notice that she had a disability. Others again wondered what I was doing there. But I know. I was like Aaron, the person who makes the prophet's words intelligible, the interpreter, the brother. It is only when Bénédicte's story is told that it acquires its full prophetic force.
So, if Bénédicte fully exercises her royal and prophetic functions,

shouldn't we do everything we can to allow her to exercise her priestly function by serving at the Lord's table?

III The common priesthood of the faithful

Vatican II's *Lumen Gentium* notes that a person's whole life is connected to the Eucharistic offering of the Lord's body (LG 34). This is the heart of the common priesthood of the faithful; there is no need to serve at the altar to exercise this priestly role. At the same time, Pope Francis specifically draws attention to the contribution every person with a disability can make to the performance of the liturgy through significant actions. Such an action could be serving at the altar. And what if God had given Bénédicte the charism of service? It is possible that for Bénédicte being a server is the means whereby the Spirit can produce his fruits in her, place her at the service of the community in order to make it grow in humanity, so that everyone realises that people with disabilities are necessary and precious members of the Church. The new priest's unease is a sign of a difficulty in discerning Bénédicte's wish to be a real charism. In October 2014 Pope Francis said this about charisms:

> *The most beautiful experience, though, is the discovery of all the different charisms and all the gifts of his Spirit that the Father showers on his Church! This must not be seen as a reason for confusion, for discomfort: they are all gifts that God gives to the Christian community, in order that it may grow in harmony, in the faith and in his love, as one body, the Body of Christ.*[11]

A charism is a grace of the Spirit that makes the community of the faithful grow in humanity by creating in them an attitude that protects them from prejudices and exclusion, encouraging the sense of being a real family and a respect for diversity as an added value. Calling for Bénédicte to have a place at the altar is not about power or any assertion of female authority. It is about the recognition of an unexpected charism, of the prophetic value of the presence at the altar of a vulnerable person whose capacity to serve the community and the Lord should be promoted by the Church. It is about unconditional acceptance, allowing Bénédicte to carry out her mission where the Lord has put her.

IV The irruption of God into our lives and the aesthetic dimension of the liturgy

A priest friend once remarked to me: 'For a long time I've had a keen sense of the aesthetic dimension of the liturgy: the row of alter-servers in albs represents a coherence, an ideal of unity.' There is certainly an aesthetic dimension to the liturgy to which the assembly of the faithful is generally sensitive: Pope Benedict XVI even discussed it in a paragraph of his Apostolic Exhortation *Sacramentum Caritatis*,[12] and the whole pastoral approach based on the *via pulchritudinis* as a path to faith testifies to this enthusiasm for beauty that leads to God. In this context the mystery of harmonious beauty is seen as pointing towards a mystery that surpasses everything. So has Bénédicte been rejected from the altar because she can't be fitted into this aesthetic coherence? In the same paragraph of *Sacramentum Caritatis* Benedict XVI warns us against a pure aestheticism: '"the fairest of the sons of men" (Ps 45[44]:3) is also, mysteriously, the one "who had no form or comeliness that we should look at him, and no beauty that we should desire him" (Is 53:2)'. The reference to 'mystery' here puts us on a different path, that of an incomprehensible dimension that transcends us and takes us where we do not want to go. This is the *via turpitudinis*, the path of hurt, of fragility and vulnerability. God also comes to us by this path in the liturgy, because the Eucharist makes possible a meeting with God in Jesus crucified and risen. At the Agnus Dei the celebrant breaks the consecrated bread and shows it to the assembly. This broken bread speaks of communion with all that is broken, God's closeness to all our fragilities, his life-giving presence at the heart of our vulnerabilities, our limitations, our defects. And yet God is not *in* the ritual; he is with the excluded people, because the world has not grasped their meaning for the Church as body-of-Christ. Ejecting Bénédicte from the altar deprives the assembly of the presence of Christ in its midst.

Allowing Bénédicte to be an altar-server might upset a an ideal vision of the liturgy or breach a certain conventional aesthetic harmony. But God is precisely in that breaching of harmony that bursts into the community. With her awkward walk and slow movements, but also with her enthusiasm and her overflowing love for the Lord, she shows in her own way how God makes the world's wisdom foolish (1 Cor 1.20). And yet again the world does not recognise divine wisdom. Yes, faith may take us along the *via pulchritudinis*, but beauty never speaks the complexity of God's mystery. We can't take refuge in beauty when we set off in search of God, because God is also in what is considered as not sharing in that beauty. We should not think that the *via turpitudinis* is empty of God. The God who reveals himself in the tortured body of a man crucified is certainly not afraid of showing himself in the uncertain gait of an elderly woman with learning difficulties. The aesthetic dimension of the liturgy is good for us with its beauty because it combines beauty and goodness,[13] but it also does us good when it welcomes fragility and hurt. Liturgy makes possible a privileged time in which God bursts into our lives, often in an unexpected way. It is a time of grace, a *kairos*.

V Conclusion

So have we got to find something else for Bénédicte to do? Could the one who invited to his banquet the poor, the crippled, the lame and the blind (Lk 14.13) refuse to let them serve at his table? Would the one who put the paralysed man back on his feet and set the blind man on the road, who demands a place for everyone in the community, feel awkward if he was served by Bénédicte? I think the answer to these questions has to be No. Theologically, there is nothing to prevent Bénédicte being a server at the celebration of the Eucharist. The difficulty is an anthropological one: it resides at the level of perceptions of disability, it has to do with the images current in our societies about ideal beauty and harmony. It is not in my power to change the way our contemporaries look at disability. But simply allow me to end this contribution with some words of Cardinal Newman: 'There are ten thousand ways of looking at this world, but only one right way.... There is but one right way; it is the way in which God looks at the world. Aim at looking at it in God's way'.[14] And when God looked at the world God saw that all God had made was truly beautiful.

Translated by Francis McDonagh

Notes

1. Etienne Grieu, 'Méthodes biographiques et théologie pratique', *Didaskalia* 39 (2009/2), 125-143.
2. Étienne Grieu, 'Méthodes biographiques et théologie pratique', 143.
3. *Redemptionis Sacramentum*, 47. The French text used by the author refers to 'children' and 'young people', whereas the Latin and the English have 'boys or youths' (*Translator*).
4. http://www.vatican.va/content/paul-vi/la/motu_proprio/documents/hf_p-vi_motu-proprio_19720815_ministeria-quaedam.html, Section VII:
'The institution of reader and acolyte, in accordance with a venerable Church tradition, is reserved to men.'
5. Hélène Bricout and Martin Klöckener, 'Des garçons et des filles au service de l'autel', *La Maison Dieu* 294 (2018/4), 145-174.
6. Sacred Congregation for the Discipline of the Sacraments, Instruction *Immensae caritatis*, of 29 January 1973, 1. V; DC 1630 (1973), p. 359.
7. *Serviteurs d'Évangile*, actes synodaux du diocèse de Poitiers, 2003, n° 3123.
8. See Anne-Marie Philippe, 'Vocations et handicaps', *Eglise et vocations*, n°1, (February 2008), 113-120.
9. http://w2.vatican.va/content/francesco/fr/speeches/2016/june/documents/papa-francesco_20160611_convegno-disabili.html (consulté le 19/02/2019).
10. Ibid.
11. Cf. FRANÇOIS, Audience générale du 1 octobre 2014, disponible sur : http://m2.vatican.va/content/francesco/fr/audiences/2014/documents/papa-francesco_20141001_udienza-generale.html (consulté le 19/06/2019).
12. Benedict XVI, Apostolic Exhortation *Sacramentum Caritatis*, 35: http://www.vatican.va/content/benedict-xvi/en/apost_exhortations/documents/hf_ben-xvi_exh_20070222_sacramentum-caritatis.html
13. Patrick Prétot, 'La liturgie et son potentiel de formation éthique', *Revue d'éthique et de théologie morale* (2008/HS), 147-62.
14. See 'Sermon 3. Unreal Words', in J. H. Newman, *Parochial and Plain Sermons*, San Francisco, CA., 1997, p. 986; also online: http://www.newmanreader.org/works/parochial/volume5/sermon3.html

Liturgical Imagination at Full Stretch: Possibilities for Leadership of Disabled People

MIRIAM SPIES

Disabled clergy are beginning to stretch leadership practices, but overall ministers with disabilities remain the "un-imagined". This paper will encourage imagination in liturgy to help disabled people lead. Imagination interrogates discriminatory practices in determining who is "perfect" enough to lead worship. Imagination helps live in liturgical time as "crip time". Imagining a person with a disability not only receiving the Eucharist but presiding at Jesus' table can affirm the existence and gifts of disabled people as well as others participating. Through stretching our imagination about leadership, time, and sacraments, the ministry of disabled people can challenge and transform the church.

Liturgical theologian Saliers writes about liturgy embodying humanity at full stretch before God and neighbour.[1] Disabled people are beginning to stretch leadership practices, but overall ministers with disabilities remain the "un-imagined" and the "essentially excluded"[2] in pastoral ministry. The church's obsession with perfection must be interrogated to reground us in who we are worshipping and why we are called to worship. Liturgical imagination can help perceive and use time in a counter-cultural way. When disabled bodies both receive and preside at the sacrament of communion, our discipleship of love, mutuality, and vulnerability can be witnessed and celebrated, and our Christian witness can be transformed. Liturgical leadership by people who continue to be excluded can serve as a subversive witness to God's kingdom on earth.

Growing up the daughter of two preachers I did not imagine becoming a minister, not because of my Cerebral Palsy, but rather because the work seemed very demanding. As a young adult I sensed a call to serve and was ordained five years ago in The United Church of Canada. As I sought ordination, I named that people's experience of me transforms once we establish a relationship, using a lens of the social model of disability, but when seeking a call, this reasoning no longer fit. People could not imagine my body in settings like liturgical spaces with all that entailed (a power wheelchair, limited fine motor skills, and affected speech). I was ordained and served in one congregation for three years, but the question of access for presiding in other congregations remains. I intend to spark the imagination and heart for justice, waiting to be borne from worshipping God together.

I Perfection and Leadership

Many believe that the identity of the minister communicates much about who the church is or wants to become. The mandate from Leviticus that said priests were to be "without blemish" (Lev. 21:16 NRSV) has barred women and queer people from ministry and continues to in many denominations. Nearly three decades ago, Herzog found that persons with disabilities were discouraged from entering ordained ministry because their "deviance" did not fit the expectations of The United Methodist Church.[3] Nowadays, the church's obsession with perfection, especially in leadership, may not be explicitly said, but is communicated in which parts of the building are accessible, the people who are serving and who are being served, and the presence of those in leadership. This messaging, regrettably, has seeped into the hearts of disabled people. While presenting about disabled leaders in the church, Fubara-Manuel encountered a person with impaired sight who asked, "Do [you] truly believe in the possibility of a blind person or crippled person serving as the moderator of the general assembly of our great church?" Prodding the question further, she found that "his worry was that a disabled moderator would be a distraction to the image and message of the church."[4] The United Church of Canada has never had a moderator with a disability, though soon after the Very Rev. Giuliano was elected he was diagnosed with cancer and underwent treatment. In writing afterwards, he recalled, "I dreamed of leading our church for a time from a place of strength, wisdom, and creativity. Instead I have been offering my weakness to the church... I would not have chosen it, but I cannot deny that it has been a gift to me and to others."[5] Perhaps if the cancer diagnosis came earlier, he would have withdrawn sensing his disability as a distraction too, instead of embodying grace and weakness as part of God's call.

The weekly liturgy is the primary public expression of the church. Jacober notes training is deemed necessary to lead, saying, "Corporate worship always seem(s) to morph from a time of responding to God to being in awe of the talents of others."[6] Liturgy should, indeed, liberate people from our culture that "denies limits and glorifies the 'perfect' body and mind."[7] In and through the liturgy another way of being can be revealed. The United Church of Canada stresses ministry of the whole people of God. "This means," writes Caron "worship, including worship leadership, belongs to the whole people of God."[8] This is very challenging to live out. When a group of United Church ministers came together to write about ministry amidst their chronic illnesses, they mourned how often they are assumed to be spectators rather than leaders or experienced as less able because they sat to preside or they were named as almost divine because of their ability to lead. "Either way," they wrote, "we are not ordinary human beings with the foibles and gifts that make us who we are as persons."[9]

The church has created liturgical boundaries in relation to leadership, but as Spurrier says, "These uneasy liturgical boundaries are also an important place for tracing the work of beauty and disability."[10] Worship can be a place of transforming our fears as well as our expectations of perfection to a space where the Body of Christ is interdependent. In her research, Fox encountered a pastor with disabilities that affect his speech and movement along with his learning abilities. As a senior pastor, "he named his disability as helping to nurture a safe and healing congregation, since he is not 'perfect' according to conventional standards."[11] Liturgy that embraces people's knowledge and experiences is full of possibilities.

Without glorifying disabled bodies or using them as tools for teaching, disabled bodies, as well as other marginalized bodies, are vital for liturgy as humanity at full stretch.[12]

An United Church congregation in Hamilton, ON, has the practice of handing out scripture readings on Sunday mornings as people come into worship. More often than not, a man in a power chair picks up a reading. As he comes to the center of the circle to read, another member reaches for the microphone and holds it in front of his mouth. Parking his wheelchair, the paper crinkles as he unfolds it. Returning to the circle he isn't the congratulated, he isn't used as a sermon metaphor, and he isn't told that he should not read every week; rather his leadership is expected, imagined, and supported. Titchkosky says, "It is thus a very strange disruption, indeed, to regard disability as key to the plan, as not only a possible participant but a desirable one."[13] By disrupting cultural and church notions of perfection, the congregation not only makes space for this man but desires his leadership amidst them. In its statement, "A Church of All and for All," the World Council of Churches affirms that disabled people challenge the culture where perfection in the worldly image is our priority, where weakness is criticized and failures concealed, rather than living into God's image.[14] Re-imagining space and time in the liturgy for disabled ministers and leaders is not only about the leaders themselves, but about the whole congregation. The WCC statement concludes: "To feel truly welcome in the church, persons with disabilities need to see people like themselves in leadership roles."[15] The bodies of disabled liturgical leaders expose the masquerade of perfection, revealing that all bodies are needed and affirmed and that interdependent practices can be imagined.

II Liturgical "Crip" Time

Disability is disruptive to the world, to people's experiences, and even to churches and their liturgical practices. One way is in the area of time. Time has become managed in our capitalist society. The gift of liturgical time is counter-cultural, as taking time for God and for others is indeed a liturgical act. Sailers reminds us that liturgy is not something to be checked off a list, but rather a transformation that takes time: "The transformative power of God's self-giving in and through liturgical action has to do with the shaping of perception, of knowing, of feeling over time."[16] For many Western mainline denominations our need to order time runs into liturgical practices. Spurrier spent a few years studying a congregation where a majority of its parishioners live with disabilities and mental health issues.

She comments that participants could be entrusted with more work of the church, including liturgical leadership, but adds, "sharing responsibility for such work would slow time [...] in ways that also disrupt efficient patterns of church gathering."[17] Like many congregations, they struggle with imagining time for all peoples to share in liturgical leadership.

Our Western experiences of keeping the worship service to an hour or of limiting the liturgy writing to one person limits involvement. Kim-Cragg writes, "The belief that worship must be decent and orderly may be behind most of [the] reluctance to change."[18] Cerebral Palsy has affected my speech. Imagining me as a presider requires congregations to imagine time differently. For some my speech begins as unintelligible, but over time becomes easier to understand. When people remark how my speech has improved, I respond that it is rather their listening that has improved. Some people tell me that my speech invites them to listen more attentively. While I strive to keep my sermons and prayers shorter, I challenge the community not to be bound by the *chronos* clock, but to live by *kairos* time. Time in becoming accustomed to how one speaks is not only an issue of disability but includes others within the full stretch of humanity. Ministers from racialized backgrounds, immigrant and Canadian-born, experience congregations complaining of not understanding their speech or citing it as a reason not to call them. If we use imagination in liturgical time, disability can disrupt capitalistic values and return us to living in God's time.[19] Working in liturgical time, we are called to settle into a different rhythm of activity and sabbath, celebration and mourning, where one is not judged by productivity, but rather is invited into deeper relationship with God, creation, and one another.

Disability activists have claimed "crip time" which as Kafer explains:

> is a flex time not just expanded but exploded; it requires reimagining our notions of what can and should happen in time, or recognizing how expectations of 'how long things take' are based on very particular minds and bodies... Rather than bend disabled bodies and minds to meet the clock, crip time bends the clock to meet disabled bodies and minds.[20]

As crip time bends the clock to meet our bodies and minds, liturgical time creates imagination for valuing different approaches to participation and leadership. A liturgy that counters society's (de)valuing of time would imagine leadership in a liturgical-crip time where leadership is not judged based on worshiping in under an hour, and where we can encounter Jesus Christ who has died, is risen, and will come again.

III Presiding at Communion or Eucharist
The whole of worship is experienced through our bodies, including the movements of the sacrament of communion. We follow Jesus as he commanded: "Take, bless, break, and pour. Do this in remembrance of me." The intentionality of these actions slows us down to be present to our relationship with Christ. The first time a minister presides at the sacrament of communion is often sacred. A couple weeks after my ordination, I presided at communion in my home congregation. Sitting in one of the pews was Rev. Seiichi Ariga, a United Church minister who studied with my parents. Following the service, with tears in his eyes, he said to me, "You were Jesus for me." Initially, I felt discomfort, as many in the church have spiritualized disabled people with damaging effects. However, upon reflection, I think he spoke to me as a minister who faced barriers in the church and society because of his Japanese heritage, one marginalized minister encountering another. My embodiment at the table made space for him to identify with the pathos of Christ and to experience the visible grace of God: "Our pathos, the reality of human life, our daily struggle to make sense of longings, hopes, fears, joys, provides an experiential link."[21] Both of our marginalized identities and bodies were welcome at the table, and in that mixture of joy, struggle, and yearning we continued to be shaped as Christians, imagining God's kingdom on earth as a place where both of our leadership gifts are not only welcome or tolerated but desired.

Many disabled people have been excluded from participating in the sacrament, let alone presiding at the table. Eisland spoke about how communion became a ritual of segregation and degradation, a solitary practice rather than a corporate one because of her inability to kneel at a rail. Sharing the story of a theologian who was denied entrance to seminary until he could perform the sacrament "appropriately", she notes, "In making the Eucharist a physical practice of exclusion, the church demonstrates a tangible bias against our nonconventional bodies and dishonours the disabled God."[22] Participating in the prayer of great thanksgiving led by a disabled minister, receiving the elements from someone with a disability, and/or accompanying disabled people receive the elements can be an act of resistance.

Postcolonial scholars, like Kim-Cragg, note how the Eucharist has the potential to be liberating or oppressive for women and other marginalized groups who have been denied both access to it and authority to officiate it. And so, she argues,

> There is a subversive performance happening when a woman priest [...] lifts up the chalice. She is denouncing authority that demonizes women's bodies and dismisses their leadership. When a transgender minister stands at the communion table having overcome the barriers of transphobia in family, church, and society, the wall of heteronormativity and gender binary is broken down.[23]

Although Kim-Cragg is speaking about gender identities, when disabled people preside at the Eucharist, there is also a subversive performance happening. I have struggled to find spaces to offer ministry, as a queer disabled woman. With the limitations of my movements, I require assistance in the actions of breaking and pouring. While some have been denied the privilege to preside due to this inability, my presence at the communion table reflects how my life, and indeed all of our lives, are interdependent and are vulnerable. When the limits of disabled people are imagined or expected, a space opens for creativity and interdependence in the liturgy. The church is called to be a place of interdependence: how we depend on God and how God depends on us, how we depend on Jesus Christ as our Teacher, as the Bread of Life and how Jesus depends on us, his disciples in anticipating and co-creating the kingdom of God as the Body of Christ.

A ministry of interdependence may sound beautiful; it is also messy and disruptive. It requires communication and trust as well as honesty about our limits and creativity in working together. Presiding at table with lay members or another ordered minister who perform the actions as I speak the words bears witness to our common humanity, our vulnerability, and thus our need for God and each other in our discipleship of Jesus. We embody the interdependent body of Christ. With humility, I hope my leadership is "an altered body practice of the Eucharist [that] is the evidence that the grace of God comes through grace. Hence, it is at once a call for justice and a recognition of the value of nonconventional bodies."[24] Those gathered are participating in this subversive act of resilience. Our words and actions must join together in this sacrament of communion, of interdependence, of justice pointing to new life and liberation.

Even without a "marginalized" presider at the table, our words in remembering the Christ who subverted systems and sought justice, the table can be one where all bodies are imagined. Though, without my Cerebral Palsy, I would not have perceived the beauty of interdependent body at Christ's table in the same way. As Robitscher reflected on her experience in ministry, "God was being mediated to them in a new way—or perhaps in an old, New Testament way. Not the perfect 'priest=Jesus' model, but the 'Disabled God.'"[25] The table bends time to fit my body, to fit the bodies of others who are enacting the words of institution, and to fit the real bodies of those who receive the gift of bread for the journey and cup of blessing. Imagining disabled people and other marginalized leaders as presiders at the table of Jesus Christ, liturgy can act as a commitment to justice, sending us forth to transform the society to be one based on solidarity and love.

In witnessing to the love of God through the broadness of humanity, liturgies can stretch our imagination so that we encounter disabled people as leaders. Psalm 40 offers both a liturgical lament and call to possibility: "I waited patiently for the Lord; he inclined to me and heard my cry... He put a new song in my mouth, a song of praise to our God. Many will see and fear, and put their trust in the Lord." (Ps. 40:1, 3) As disabled leaders seek to praise God with congregations, imagination around expectations of leadership, time as well as the call to be fed and sent forth will be expanded. I am heartened by the possibilities of liturgical imagination for every body's leadership. Congregations as contextualized settings should be investigated further as age, race, gender, sexual orientations, and other identities help shape imaginations. Let us continue to be stretched into possibility and transformation, where disabled leaders are imagined and expected, for the sake of God's love.

Notes

1. Don Saliers, "Toward a Spirituality of Inclusiveness," in *Human Disability and the Service of God: Reassessing Religious Practice*, ed. Nancy Eiesland and Don Saliers (Nashville, TN: Abingdon Press, 1998), 28.
2. Tanya Titchkosky, *The Question of Access: Disability, Space, Meaning* (Toronto: University of Toronto Press, Scholarly Publishing Division, 2011), 39.
3. Albert Herzog, "'We Have This Ministry': Ordained Ministers Who Are Physically Disabled," in *Human Disability and the Service of God: Reassessing Religious Practice*, ed. Don Saliers and Nancy Eiesland (Nashville: Abingdon Press, 1998), 187-199, here 188.
4. Jessie Fubara☐Manuel, "Together with All the Saints: Journeying with Persons with Disabilities," in *Walking Together: Theological Reflections on the Ecumenical Pilgrimage of Justice and Peace*, ed. Susan Durber and Fernando Enns (Geneva: WCC Publications, 2018), 101-110, here 103.
5. David Giuliano, *Postcards From the Valley* (Toronto: United Church Publishing House, 2008), 1.
6. Amy E. Jacober, *Redefining Perfect: The Interplay Between Theology and Disability* (Eugene, Oregon: Cascade Books, an Imprint of Wipf and Stock Publishers, 2018), 68.
7. Don Saliers, "Toward a Spirituality of Inclusiveness," in *Human Disability and the Service of God: Reassessing Religious Practice*, ed. Nancy Eiesland and Don Saliers (Nashville, TN: Abingdon Press, 1998), 19-31, here 29.
8. Charlotte Caron, *Eager for Worship: Theologies, Practices, and Perspectives on Worship in the United Church of Canada* (Toronto: Division of Ministry Personnel and Education, United Church of Canada, 2000), 204.
9. Charlotte Caron and Barb Wire Collective, eds., *Not All Violins: Spiritual Resources by Women with Disabilities and Chronic Illnesses* (Toronto: United Church Pub, 1997), 173.
10. Rebecca F. Spurrier, *The Disabled Church: Human Difference and the Art of Communal Worship* (New York: Fordham University Press, 2019), 209.
11. Bethany McKinney Fox, *Disability and the Way of Jesus* (Downers Grove: IVP Academic, 2019), 119.
12. See Nancy Eiesland, *The Disabled God* (Nashville: Abingdon Press, 1994), 115.
13. Titchkosky, *The Question of Access: Disability, Space, Meaning*, 34.
14. World Council of Churches, "A Church of All and for All," (Geneva: WCC Publications, 2003), 12
15. World Council of Churches, "A Church of All and for All," 15
16. Don Saliers, *Worship As Theology* (Nashville: Abingdon Press, 1994), 283.
17. Spurrier, *The Disabled Church*, 119.
18. HyeRan Kim-Cragg, *Interdependence: A Postcolonial Feminist Practical Theology*. (Eugene, Oregon: Pickwick Publications, an Imprint of Wipf and Stock Publishers, 2018), 72.
19. See John Swinton, *Becoming Friends of Time: Disability, Timefullness, and Gentle Discipleship* (Waco, Texas: Baylor University Press, 2016), 82.
20. Alison Kafer, *Feminist, Queer, Crip* (Bloomington: Indiana University Press, 2013), 27.
21. Don Saliers, "Human Pathos and Divine Ethos," in *Primary Sources of Liturgical Theology: A Reader*, ed. Dwight Vogel (Collegeville, MN: The Liturgical Press, 2000), 278.

22. Eiesland, *The Disabled God*, 113.
23. HyeRan Kim-Cragg, "Postcolonial Practices on Eucharist," in *Postcolonial Practice of Ministry: Leadership, Liturgy, and Interfaith Engagement*, ed. Stephen Burns and Pui-lan Kwok (New York: Lexington Books, 2016), 86-87.
24. Eiesland, *The Disabled God*, 115.
25. Jan Robitscher, "Through Glasses Darkly: Discovering a Liturgical Place," in *Human Disability and the Service of God: Reassessing Religious Practice*, ed. Nancy Eiesland and Don Saliers (Nashville: Abingdon Press, 1998), 144-164, here 154.

Relationships of Solidarity as Heterotopias bringing Wholeness to People with (and without) Disabilities

MARTIN M. LINTNER

After some terminological preliminaries about the description of people with a disability, the article stresses that we are dealing first and foremost with people, people who cope with their lives, their relationships, and their inclusion in society under the particular condition of their disability, and that society often does not support them in this, but instead puts obstacles in their way. The article interprets disability as giving particular visibility to vulnerability as the human condition and the need, shared by all human beings, for redemption. Even when the desire for cure and healing is intelligible, where in medical and therapeutic terms healing is unlikely, disabilities must be accepted. This leads to a critical deconstruction of ideas of health and perfection. Unrealistic expectations and utopian hopes must not be nurtured, but inclusion must be practised as a process for creating a society of solidarity as a 'healing heterotopia'.

I An introductory remark on terminology

You could fill volumes with the discussions about how people with a disability – whether physical, psychological or intellectual - should be described. They often become controversial and emotional. I offer three short reflections as an introduction to the topic of the article.

(a) Terms such as 'disabled' or 'disabled person', or even 'person with a disability/limitation' are today often felt to be discriminating and pejorative. One argument is that the people concerned are being reduced linguistically to a feature of their individual human existence, which in addition is described as a defect. Alternative terms are put forward, such as 'person with special abilities/needs' or 'otherwise abled person'. But these options also face criticism. People concerned, we are told, are still in practice confronted with disadvantages in our society, their 'special abilities' are hardly recognised as such socially, let alone valued. Their 'special needs' or being 'otherwise' abled and so on is in practice often associated with restrictions, and the terms in question are therefore euphemistic and trivialising.

(b) The arguments about terminology are unavoidable. However, they should not mislead us into thinking that new or alternative terminology on its own will solve the problem. Much more important, of course, is that we deal with the people concerned in such a way that the limitation they have does not prevent them from developing in accordance with their abilities, possibilities and personal ideas, shaping their lives within the degree of autonomy open to them, being involved in relationships and taking part in the life of society. Disability Studies differentiates between the physical, psychological or intellectual dimensions of a disability on the level of an individual's medical condition and disability in the sense of the social effects of this limitation, which may range from prejudice about those affected and dismissal of them to their stigmatisation and exclusion. People affected may be disabled not (only) by physical, psychological or intellectual characteristics, but (even more) by a range of social obstacles and difficulties, including the way other people and society see them and behave towards them. Discussion of how the people affected are spoken about and spoken to is necessary to overcome negative stereotypes and expose the way terminologies, concepts and meanings applied to disability in society in general, politics and culture affect them. This includes whether they are valued and respected – or not, whether they are supported and enabled and whether they are given the chance of shaping their lives independently in accordance with their possibilities and abilities and to develop as people – or the reverse.[1]

(c) This article adopts (except in quotations) the term 'human beings with a disability'. This is intended to emphasise that they are first and foremost human beings, who have the same dignity and the same human rights as all human beings. At the same time they live and exercise their humanity under the particular condition of a disability, with all its social effects. This has to be recognised and stated, so that we can do greater justice to the specific needs and abilities of these human beings and more effectively include them in the community to which we all belong.[2] The choice of this term is intended to indicate a limitation or disability, but not to reduce the person affected by it to that disability. Conversely, genuine differences and particular challenges that a life with a disability entails cannot be glossed over by new linguistic usages.

II Disability, vulnerability and relatedness

Human beings with a disability exercise their humanity under the particular condition of their disability, which has effects both on the individual and the social level. This has consequences for encounters with them.

(a) They force other people and society to engage with them and to question the various ideas they hold about being human, normality or a fulfilled life. They call in question individual and social ideas, often deeply rooted and regarded as 'normal', about what a successful human life should look like, or implicit, often unexamined criteria for judging normality. 'Our ideas of normality have to do with norms, with values and so with value judgments. What constitutes the value of a person therefore does not depend on their own characteristics, but on the values we apply to them.'[3] Consequently we have to radically review 'our habits and values, which we simply regard as given. We must not look "objectively" at a person and their characteristics, but at what goes on in us, quite subjectively, in our encounter with this person.'[4]

(b) In a human being with a disability I am being met by a human being in whom vulnerability as the essential human condition is particularly visible.[5] This involves 'both the painful, suffering dimensions of human life, for example, illness and violence, and also the fulfilling dimensions, such as love and trust.'[6] Heike Springhart differentiates between ontological vulnerability, which is common to all human beings, and the conditions in which it is experienced, which depend on the individual situation.[7] Subjective reactions to an encounter with a human being with disability therefore relate not just to ideas about human life or normality, but essentially also to the way one deals with the vulnerability that is the lot of all human beings, which takes a different form, and is experienced and dealt with differently in each case. The crucial factor is that our dealings with a human being with a disability should be guided by their individual situation, their idea and own sense of themselves and their experience of life, not by our own or society's ideas of normality.

(c) Every human being relies to a different degree on help, care and attention. This need and dependence of a human being for and on others, this relatedness and reliance on others, does not reduce their dignity. In the Judeo-Christian view, it is instead part of a human being's make-up as a created being, and it is by the way that mutual, especially asymmetrical, relationships are structured that the humanity of an individual or a society is measured. This means that we must distinguish between a view of autonomy in which 'a human being is understood as in principle or potentially an agent who acts autonomously, which is what leads to the idea of the feasibility of a successful life,'[8] and self-determination as critically differentiated from a life determined by others, which amounts to tutelage and blocks maturity. The dealings we have to have with human beings with a disability, however, act as a 'fracture' in the image of the ideal human being in which autonomy, independence, performance, health, freedom from suffering, etc. are the dominant features.

III The wish for a fulfilled life

A longing for a fulfilled and successful life, hope for health and an unimpaired life, like vulnerability and relatedness, can be regarded as an aspect of the human condition. 'The desire for healing, especially when it is expressed by people who are chronically ill or people with a disability, is all too understandable… Sick and disabled people hope that new treatments or rehabilitation programmes will bring them, if not healing, at least advances and an improvement in their lived situation.'[9]

(a) In this connection Wolfgang Reuter indicates an important challenge and introduces an important change of perspective. It is in particular chronic invalids and people with a disability who have to come to terms with and accept, indeed reconcile themselves with, the fact that despite their longing for healing and despite the possibilities and the efforts made by medicine and therapies, they will not find an easing, a cure or healing, but will have to live with illness or disability. Reuter argues that this makes it important, while we must take seriously the longing for a cure, not to reproduce the ideals of health and wholeness and the expectations and hopes bound up with them. Instead, in accompanying people with a disability, the 'experience of suffering as the basic and contrasting experience of healthy, disabled and sick people must be the focus'.[10] Instead of 'healing' or 'therapeutic', he talks about 'what makes whole'. 'What makes whole' turns out to be accompaniment and pastoral care for human beings with a disability in the sense of being consistently on the side of these human beings, taking serious their experiences of suffering, their sense of themselves and their longing for a fulfilled life.

(b) As a basis in biblical theology for this approach to pastoral care focused on wholeness, Reuter points to the saving mystery of Christ, which includes the experience of suffering on the cross, but also the hope of the resurrection. Sickness and disability must not be either trivialised or romanticised in a mystique of suffering. Nevertheless, where easing or healing are not possible, they do reveal, not only the normal state of vulnerability that is the human condition, but also the hope of redemption that comes from the Christian faith. Every human being is in need of redemption and lives in the tension identified by the theological term 'eschatological reservation', namely that we have already been redeemed by Christ, but the fullness of redemption is yet to come. This Christian hope is not intended to be a consolation strategy, but a source that provides motivation and gives strength to endure life with its experiences of not yet being redeemed.

(c) According to the testimony of the gospels, Jesus encountered many people who suffered from a disease or disability and healed them. The crucial factor, however, is that in these stories the main feature is not the healing in the sense of a miracle or the demonstration of Jesus' special medical abilities, but that the healed people benefit from Jesus' unlimited attention.[11] In many cases these are people whose illness or disability has left them stigmatised, excluded and as a result extremely vulnerable. Healing becomes possible as unquestioned ideas of normality and categories of difference are deconstructed, so that diversity and difference are recognised as legitimate. People who are different because of a disease or disability are not excluded, but brought into the community. Jesus addresses himself to them without reserve and without prejudice, and creates community with them. His interpretative categories are not social or religious ideas of normality and health, but rather the testimony that in the eyes of God every human being is valuable and loved and yet in need of redemption.

In this perspective differences between human beings no longer make any difference at all or do not count when the important thing is to create community and live in relationship. As regards human beings with a disability above all, the essential thing is not physical or mental healing, but making God's love accessible by overcoming exclusion and through processes of integration. Such experiences bring wholeness particularly where they nurture hope of redemption: a hope that is not empty optimism, but which helps people to process experiences of disability they have lived and suffered so that they create a sensibility for a deeper, often hidden meaning of every life that is lived.

IV A society of solidarity as a heterotopia that brings wholeness

While it is completely justified to long for relief and healing, and without prejudice to the phenomenon of unexpected cures with no medical explanation that the Church regards as miracles, in many cases of physical, mental or psychological disability, despite every effort and when all real medical or other therapeutic possibilities have been exhausted, a cure seems unlikely and beyond expectation – and in this sense utopian. Here there is a need for extreme caution not to encourage unrealistic expectations or nurture utopian hopes.

In contrast to utopias, Michel Foucault coined the term 'heterotopias'. These are: 'real places, actual places, places designed as part of the very institution of society, which are a sort of counter-site, a sort of utopias actually brought about in which the real sites, all the other real sites to be found within culture, are represented, challenged and at the same time inverted, the sorts of places that are outside all places, even though they are nevertheless actually locatable'.[12]

In a society in which all members actively collaborate in the creation of relationships of solidarity,[13] and no-one tries to get out of it by saying there are specialised services that can deal with every sort of emergency,[14] this sort of heterotopia can be created in this process. The focus here is not miraculous cures that medicine can't explain at particular places (such as Lourdes, etc.) – as a sort of privilege for a chosen few – but the relationships between all people (with and without disability) at all places. The guiding principle is inclusion, that is the integration 'by all means relevant to the person, starting with the planning. People with disabilities should be represented in the relevant steering groups and should as far as possible represent their own interests. But in doing so they should not be left to their own devices, but receive all possible support, and this should be offered as early as possible, especially in the form of inclusive educational opportunities, but lifelong.'[15] In this way they will be encouraged and enabled to shape their lives as they decide, within the limits of their possibilities, and to help to shape the society they are part of. Differences that exist will not be seen as defects and will not be an obstacle to a person in their uniqueness and vulnerability, with their individual needs and abilities, being recognised and valued.

Translated by Francis McDonagh

Notes

1. On this see: Stefano Semplici, 'Disability: what words to live (with) it?,' in Marie-Jo Thiel (ed.), Ethische Fragen der "Behinderung". Ethical Challanges of Disability (Symposion – Towards an Interdisciplinary Understanding 13), Münster, 2014, pp 27–41; Luisa Borgia and Giampiero Griffo, 'The bioethical approach towards persons with disabilities. A new idea of justice, in Marie-Jo Thiel, Ethische Fragen der "Behinderung". Ethical Challanges of Disability , pp 43–61; Bernhard Joss-Dubach, Gegen die Behinderung des Andersseins. Ein theologisches Plädoyer für die Vielfalt von Menschen mit einer geistigen Behinderung, Zürich: , 2014, pp 479–484.
2. See Maria Zanichelli, *Persone prima che disabili. Una riflessione sull'handicap tra giustizia ed etica* (*Nuovi Saggi Querinana* 89), Brescia, 2012.
3. Walter Lorenz, '"Geistig behindert – na und?" Inklusion als Anerkennung und Wertschätzung,' in: *Beiheft zum Brixner Theologischen Jahrbuch* 9 (2018), Brixen, 2019, 13-18, esp. 14–15.
4. Lorenz, '"Geistig behindert – na und?,"' 15.
5. Zanichelli, *Persone prima che disabili*, pp 77–86; Heike Springhart, 'Inklusion und Vulnerabilität – systematisch-theologische Überlegungen,' in Michaela Geiger and Matthias Stracke-Barholmai (ed.), *Inklusion denken. Theologisch, biblisch, ökumenisch, praktisch (Behinderung – Theologie – Kirche. Beiträge zu diakonisch-caritativen Disability Studies* 10), Stuttgart, 2018, pp 33–42.
6. Springhart, 'Inklusion und Vulnerabilität', p. 35.
7. See Springhart, 'Inklusion und Vulnerabilität', p. 33.
8. Springhart, 'Inklusion und Vulnerabilität', p. 35.
9. Wolfgang Reuter, 'Heilsame Seelsorge', in Johannes Eurich and Andreas Lob-Hüdepohl (ed.), I*nklusive Kirche (Behinderung – Theologie – Kirche. Beiträge zu diakonisch-*

caritativen Disability Studies 1), Stuttgart, 2011, pp 163–170, quotation p. 165.
10. Reuter, 'Heilsame Seelsorge', p. 166.
11. See the essays in Wolfgang Grünstäudl and Markus Schiefer Ferrari (ed.), *Gestörte Lektüre: Disability als hermeneutische Leitkategorie biblischer Exegese (Behinderung – Theologie – Kirche. Beiträge zu diakonisch-caritativen Disability Studies 4)*, Stuttgart, 2012; and Markus Schiefer Ferrari, *Exklusive Angebote : biblische Heilungsgeschichten inklusiv gelesen*, Ostfildern, 2017.
12. Michel Foucault, 'Des espaces autres Hétérotopies', lecture to the Cercle d'études architecturales, 14 March 1967, in *Architecture, Mouvement, Continuité*, no 5 (1984), 46-49 : available on line in French and English at : https://foucault.info/documents/heterotopia/foucault.heteroTopia.fr (Retranslated from the French).
13. Solidarity is understood here as John Paul II used it, not as 'a feeling of vague compassion or shallow distress at the misfortunes of so many people, both near and far', but as 'a firm and persevering determination to commit oneself to the common good; that is to say to the good of all and of each individual, because we are all really responsible for all' (*Sollicitudo rei socialis* 38).
14. See Lorenz, 'Geistig behindert – na und?', p. 18.
15. Lorenz, p. 17.

Part Five: Theological Forum

Sacraments for a Sick World: Thoughts on Sacramental Lockdown During the Pandemic

MARGARETA GRUBER

The pandemic that is changing our world in unpredictable ways is still far from over. Rich countries like mine are already preparing for rebuilding the economy after, or even during, the pandemic, while in other countries they are still digging graves.

Interpretations, even religious ones, die on the lips. The virus destroys life; there is no 'deeper meaning' here. What we have to do is all that is humanly possible to combat it, to combine the efforts of science, the economy and politics to find a vaccine and make it available to all, to absolutely everyone.

The pandemic reveals the inequality in our world and its injustices, and will deepen them. The brutal exposure of racism, not just in United States society, is the example shocking the world as I write these lines (June 2020). The longing for solidarity that bore so much encouraging fruit at the beginning of the pandemic is in danger of fading away in the face of such terrible realities.

In this period many people have been sharing 'their' key pandemic moments. This is an attempt at least to give a very personal meaning to what they have felt in an experience of helplessness. In my case it was an experience that led me to think beyond the borders of the German situation. I have friends in Qom in Iran and, because people there are having a very difficult time, partly because of the sanctions imposed on the country, I wrote to them and told them about the campaign to put a candle in one's window and pray. In return I received a photo of a set of prayer beads and a candle burning for me during evening prayer in Qom. My reply was, while I joined in the televised liturgy from the Limburg bishop's chapel, to put out a candle with my rosary, pray for the people in Iran and send my photo to Qom. I couldn't help thinking, and it's a thought that filled me with deep joy: the body of Christ is much more than my Church; it includes the whole of humanity. And in these days it shows itself to us vulnerable and in mutual dependence. Healing for this wounded body must also touch all, or it will touch none.

Prophetic voices do not set out to interpret, but point to spaces that open up in the midst of a dramatic situation, spaces for making decisions. In my search for such voices I came across two that helped me to reset my compass in the crisis.

The first was the voice of Pope Francis, praying on the evening of 27 March in a deserted St Peter's Square in front of a rain-spattered plague cross: 'We carried on undaunted in the belief that in a sick world we would always stay healthy. Now, as the sea rages, we beg you, "Wake up, Lord!"' The pope said that the pandemic made us realise that 'no-one is saved by their own efforts'. That applies for all the acts of service and sacrifice performed during the pandemic, but also for the reconstruction afterwards. It also applies to the renewal of the Church.

The second voice that I felt to be prophetic came from post-Christian Prague. In an essay 'Christianity in Times of Sickness',[1] Tomáš Halík suggests: 'Perhaps this time of empty churches shows symbolically their hidden emptiness and a possible future that might begin if the churches do not seriously try to present to the world a form of Christianity that looks totally different.'[2] Conversely, he suggests that this 'state of emergency' could also be a pointer to a different sort of Church. Halík has argued for years that Christians should follow their Lord, who wants to go out of the Church and be with the seekers of our time. These seekers, Halík says, are today's Galilee, where the risen Lord sent his disciples as witnesses.

On the evening of 27 March the Pope did not, as is usual, bless the world from high on the balcony of St Peter's, but came across the threshold of the Church with the eucharistic Lord as though he wanted to go with him out into the dark and deserted city to the people shut in their homes. The media presentation of this highly symbolic ritual gave the impression, whether deliberately or not, of a sacramental general absolution for humanity in its agony.

The precise Latin proclamation of the indulgence was left in the background. The Pope stepped out in front of the doors of St Peter's as the sirens of the Roman ambulances blended with the solemn peals of the bells, and raised the monstrance in a powerful gesture of healing and forgiveness.

When I saw these images I was sitting at home in a quarantine ordered by the health authorities, because I had been in contact with an infected person. I cannot forget the fear in the first days of a possible outbreak of the disease. Perhaps that's why the blessing from Rome affected me so strongly. The powerful sign of God's presence touched my body forcefully and filled my soul with consolation. I was so grateful to God for the possibility that exists in my Church to reach people not just by word but also, even if only through a screen, sacramentally.

There followed the long weeks of 'sacramental fasting', as the period of closed churches was often called, though it was not a voluntary fast. The faithful spent hours on various sorts of streamed services; for Catholics these were mainly celebrations of the eucharist, but there were also other sorts of digital prayer meetings, often ecumenical and across national boundaries. Locally, too, as far as social distancing allowed, there were house liturgies and other sorts of prayer and celebration at which lay people, often unexpectedly, found themselves presiding.

Since then there has been discussion in Church media about what to make of these experiences. Are they the beginning of a new mode of digital presence of the Church in people's lives, in other words, the going out from the church with Christ that Halík talks about? Or was it a more or less successful emergency support service in a time of closed churches until we could as soon as possible restore the Sunday obligation and get back to 'normality'? What image of the Church do these streamed celebrations convey? Are they not characterised by an excessive concentration on the action of the priest and not always only the result of inadequate technical capacity, but a reinforcement of a sacralised image of the priest associated with the exercise of power? Where is the image of the liturgy as the action of the people of God? Through the forced focussing on the actions of the priest, many laity suddenly became aware how heavily their sacramental 'care' depends on ordained ministers. More strongly than in normal liturgical actions, one could feel who had 'access' to the sacraments and who did not. The multiplication of streamed liturgies, arranged for pastoral reasons, tended to strengthen this impression, as did the way the eucharist was distributed to the laity outside the liturgy in many places. Who do the sacraments 'belong to'? And who 'administers' them on behalf of the Church? Finding that the instruments of classical pastoral ministry were suddenly no longer available, and were also not adequate in the new situation, showed the need for a diaconal Church in a broad sense: a Church that puts its relationship with the world into practice in a new, more credible way, which will then shape the theology of Church ministry. In this way the experience of the laity's being withdrawn from the sacraments led many religious analysts, bishops as well as lay people, to call for the ordination of married men as priests and to a clear view that women should be given more tasks and ministries. What significance should we attach against this background to the house churches formed for Easter 2020? An emergency response or a return to the origins? We know, of course, that men very early took over the role of presiding at the eucharist, but what was the situation in the small house churches in Roman towns before Christianity became the established religion? We know too little about this.

After the abuse crisis, the pandemic may become the second great sign of the times that will point the Church's way into the future. The 'field hospital' reflects the pain and longing of a sick world. In the wake of the Council and in the light of a pandemic that suddenly seems to be like a huge image of humanity's situation, a new understanding of sacramentality in a diaconal Church becomes conceivable, as the dogmatic theologian Margit Eckholt puts it: 'as a relational event, action and Church practice... that grows out of God's call in a living and dynamic interaction in the people of God and is at their service. The primary purpose of the sacramental action is to make the merciful, healing and liberating action of Jesus Christ "present", wherever distress cries to heaven and people need to be given strength.'[3]

Since the time of the early Church, martyrs have been regarded as the highest form of representation of Christ. On the evening of 27 March the Pope remembered the people 'who have responded to fearful situations by giving their lives' and naturally included women. Public mentions of these people, such as cleaners or carers, by politicians and in the media, suddenly described as 'relevant to the system', were often accompanied by the comment that they were 'invisible' and regarded as 'ordinary', but that this did not reflect their significance. If only these much applauded words would be followed by deeds! But what significance are we to give to the 'relevance to the system' of women in the Church when we are not allowed to assess their giving of their lives as in the full sense representation of Christ? In Church language women's value is increased by references to the existence of Mary as a servant. This rhetoric increasingly reminds me of the bad conscience politicians have about the 'everyday heroines'. The arguments discussed amid controversy in the theology of ministry are not theologically convincing, which is why the discussion does not stop, despite pronouncements from the magisterium. Can only male bodies represent Christ's priestly role? Mary is seen as a model of the Church as bride in contrast to the male priest as the representative of Christ. But does Mary today perhaps want to be a model for priestly existence in a diaconal Church to which both men and women are called? Undoubtedly, no-one, neither man nor woman, has a 'right' to a ministry. When female voices from time to time assert this right, they are going too far. Nevertheless, they have the right to expect that their vocations will be tested. This not something that is primarily a matter of justice, but concerns the central task of the Church, as Pope Francis put it forcefully in his sermon before the great blessing: that task is to bring people the Gospel, the Easter message of hope. This needs people who can bring God into the wounded world, as Mary did, as men and women, and sacramentally.

So how am I to interpret that moving sign displayed on the evening of 27 March, the blessing on the sick world? Is it a further powerful confirmation of priestly authority in the hand of a male functionary who has the sacramental Lord in his grasp? Or is it a first step of this sacramental Lord out of the closed space of the Church into the suffering world that longs for him and feels bitter sorrow at being deprived of his presence? Where and how does he want to be made sacramentally present there? And who is allowed to take him there as a priest?

Translated by Francis McDonagh

Margareta Gruber

Notes

1. http://www.theologie-und-kirche.de/halik-theologie-pandemie.pdf
2. Halík, 2.
3. See Margit Eckholt, *Frauen in der Kirche. Zwischen Entmächtigung und Ermächtigung*, Würzburg, 2020. See also M. Eckholt, U. Link-Wieczorek, D. Sattler, A. Strübing (ed.), *Frauen in kirchlichen Ämtern. Reformbewegungen in der Ökumene*, Freiburg, 2018.

Contributors

JOHANNES S. (HANS) REINDERS, a professor of ethics and the Bernard Lievegoed Professor of Ethics and Mental Disability at the Free University of Amsterdam, has written extensively on the theological and philosophical foundations of caring for cognitively impaired persons. Through participation in international colloquia and lectures on three continents, he has contributed to the academic and public discussion of ethical issues related to disability in light, especially, of advances in genetic understanding and technologies for intervention in human development. He published several articles on disability studies from a theological perspective, between his books: *The Future of the Disabled in Liberal Society: An Ethical Analysis*, University of Notre Dame Press 2000; *and Receiving the Gift of Friendship*, Eerdmans 2008.
  Address: Warmenbossenweg 3 - 33, 9443 TN Schoonloo, Holland
  Email: j.s.reinders@vu.nl

VERONICA DONATELLO is a guest lecturer, and author of many publications and articles; she works in formation, as well as being Co-ordinator of the Italian Bishops' Conference National Service for the pastoral care of people with disabilities.
  Address: CEI – Servizio Nazionale per la Pastorale delle persone con disabilità - Circonvallazione Aurelia, 50 - 00165 Roma RM, Italy
  Email: v.donatello@chiesacattolica.it

PROFESSOR DR THEOL. MARKUS SCHIEFER FERRARI has been professor of Catholic Theology at the University of Koblenz-Landau, Landau Campus, since 2007, focusing on biblical theology, New Testament exegesis and teaching the bible. He has published on hermeneutics and teaching based on reception aesthetics, and accessible theological bible interpretation for children and Dis/ability as key categories in biblical

Contributors

exegesis.
Address: Institut für Katholische Theologie, FB 6: Kultur- und Sozialwissenschaften der Universität Koblenz-Landau (Campus Landau),
Fortstr. 7, D-76829 Landau,
Germany
Email: schiefer@uni-laudau.de

LUCA BADETTI, PhD in Disability Studies (University of Illinois at Chicago), has a background in Clinical Psychology (MS) and Theology (BA). He is the Coordinator of Service Learning and First Year Experience at Loyola University Chicago's John Felice Rome Center, where he teaches theology. He created and taught courses in disability theology (Catherine of Siena College at the University of Roehampton) and Disability Studies (DePaul University). He did research at UIC's Institute on Disability and Human Development, provided therapy at Chicago's Developmental Disabilities Family Clinic and was a LEND (Leadership Educationin Neurodevelopmental and Related Disabilities) fellow. He has been involved with international L'Arche communities for years, including as Director of Community Life at L'Arche Chicago and as Inclusion Team co-chair for L'Arche USA. He shared from what he learned in community as a published author, TEDx speaker and community consultant.
Address: Loyola University Chicago John Felice Rome Center - Via Massimi, 114/A, 00136 Rome, Italy
Email: luca@lucabadetti.com

REV. DR. HUANG PO HO is the director of the "Academy for Contextual Theologies in Taiwan" He is also teaching at Chang Jung Christian University as an adjunct professor of Theology. He was serving as vice president and professor of Theology at Chang Jung Christian University, Taiwan. And was head of the Tainan Theological College and Seminary. He served as Associate General Secretary and director of Research and Development Center of the Presbyterian Church in Taiwan; Moderator of Council for World Mission, London; Dean of the Programme for Theology and Cultures in Asia (PTCA); Moderator of the Asian Forum for Theological Education (AFTE) and Co-moderator of Congress of Asian Theologians (CATS). Dr. Huang Po Ho is a Taiwanese

Contributors

theologian deeply involving in contextual theological construction and ecumenical ministries. His numerous books include, *A Theology of Self-determination, From Galilee to Tainan, No Longer a Stranger, Mission from the Underside and Embracing the Household of God.*

Address: No. 6-5, Ln. 685, Xiaodong Rd.,Yongkang District, Tainan City 710, Taiwan (R.O.C.)

Email: cjcupekho@gmail.com

ANNE MASTERS is the Director of Office for Pastoral Ministry with Persons with Disabilities for the Archdiocese of Newark, a PhD student in Theology at Vrei University, Amsterdam, a member of the National Catholic Partnership on Disability Council on Intellectual and Developmental Disabilities, and has published and presented on the intersection of theology, disability and pastoral practices.

Address: Archdiocese of Newark, 171 Clifton Avenue, Newark, NJ 07104 USA

Email: anna.masters@rcan.org

STEPHEN ARULAMPALAM — "My education comes from experience," Stephen Arulampalam pointed out in an interview, referring to Sri Lanka's prolonged civil war and the violence, displacement, and imprisonment that he and family members experienced during those years of conflict. Given that background, perhaps it is not surprising that his interests as a theologian and ordained minister have focused on bridging the differences between Sri Lankans of Christian and Hindu faith traditions. "Theological education helps us to understand the nature of Christ's actions in our own context," he said, and in his theological studies, he has searched for a relevant Christology for Sri Lanka's post-war context. His current positions as lecturer in church history and chaplain at the Theological College of Lanka, came from his earlier work in facilitating conflict resolution seminars for Tamil and Sinhalese youth and training laypersons in dealing with post-war trauma, from scholarly writing on topics such as reconciliation and non-violent approaches toward peace.

Address: Rev. Stephen Arulampalam, Theological College of Lanka, Nandana Uyana, Pilimathalawa, Sri Lanka, 20450

Email: arulampalamstephen@gmail.com

Contributors

NAEIMEH POURMOHAMMADI is Assistant Professor of Philosophy of Religion in University of Religions and Denominations in Qom, Iran. She has PhD of Islamic Philosophy and Kalam from Science and Research Branch of Islamic Azad University in Tehran, Iran. She is interested in Problem of Evil and has many publications on it in Persian. Disability Study is her another main field of study.
  Tel: +98 25 32802609-12
  Email: n.purmohammadi@urd.ac.ir

BERNHARD NITSCHE — 2001 awarded a doctorate in theology in Tübingen for a thesis on Richard Schaeffler und Karl Rahner; 2003 awarded a doctorate in philosophy with a thesis on finitude and freedom in the context of late modernity; 2006 awarded the status of professor in Tübingen with a thesis on Raimon Pannikar's Trinitarian ideas; 2015 Professor of philosophy of religion and fundamental theology at the Westfälische Wilhelms-Universität Münster; 2007 left severely disabled by an accident.
  Address: Seminar für Fundamentaltheologie und Religionsphilosophie, Johannisstraße 8-10, D-48143 Münster, Germany
  Email: fb2fth@uni-muenster.de

DR. SAMUEL GEORGE (Th. D) is Professor of Christian Theology at Allahabad Bible Seminary (Serampore University), India. Since 2007 he is a member of the Reference Group of EDAN-WCC.
  Address: Allahabad Bible Seminary, 60/64 Stanley Road, Prayagraj, Uttar Pradesh, India, 211002
  Email: samueljammu@gmail.com

TALITHA COOREMAN-GUITTIN is a researcher at the Catholic University of Louvain. She is examining the appropriateness of maintaining friendships with people affected by Alzheimer's and the possible resources to be found in Christian spirituality to maintain these connections. Her doctoral thesis was about the perception of learning difficulties in catechesis.
  Address: Faculté de théologie, Grand'Place 45, L3.01.02, 1348 Louvain-la-neuve, Belgium
  Email: talitha.cooreman@uclouvain.be

Contributors

MIRIAM SPIES is currently pursuing a PhD at Emmanuel College, a member of the Toronto School of Theology at the University of Toronto. Her studies concentrate on supporting disabled leaders and their congregations in ministry. She is an ordained minister in The United Church of Canada. Spies lives with Cerebral Palsy.
   Address: 144 Hatton Drive, Ancaster, ON, L9G 2H6
   Email Address: miriam.spies@gmail.com

MARTIN M. LINTNER — Born 1972 in the South Tirol, Italy, studied in the theological faculties of Innsbruck, Vienna and Rome. Member of the Servite order. Professor of Moral Theology and Spiritual Theology at the Philosophisch-Theologisches Hochschule, Brixen, Italy.
   Address: Philosophisch-Theologische Hochschule Brixen, Seminarplatz 4, 39042 Brixen, Italy
   Email: martin.lintner@hs-itb.it

MARGARETA GRUBER OSF was born in 1961 in Germany. She did her studies in Tübingen, Jerusalem and Frankfurt/Sankt Georgen. She has been a Franciscan since 1989. Since 2008 she has held the Chair of New Testament Exegesis and Biblical Theology in the Faculty of Catholic Theology at the University of Vallendar, near Koblenz, Germany, where she is currently Dean. From 2009 to 2013 she led the ecumenical study programme at the Abbey of the Dormition in Jerusalem as holder of the Laurentius Klein Chair of Biblical and Ecumenical Theology. Her field of research covers the Gospel of John, the Book of Revelation, biblical hermeneutics, intertextuality, exegesis and biblical spirituality. Since her time in Jerusalem her field of interest has widened to include the bible in interreligious contexts; she is engaged in academic interreligious exchange, for example with universities in Iran.
   Address: Lehrstuhl für Exegese des Neuen Testaments und Biblische Theologie, Katholisch-Theologische Fakultät, Philosophisch-Theologische Hochschule Vallendar, Pallottistraße 3, D 56179 Vallendar, Germany
   Email: mgruber@pthv.de

Concilium Subscription Information

February   2021/1: *Church in the Borders*

April   2021/2: *Synodality*

July   2021/3: *Incarnation*

October   2021/4: *Amazons/Congo*

December   2021/5: *End of Life*

New subscribers: to receive the next five issues of Concilium please copy this form, complete it in block capitals and send it with your payment to the address below. Alternatively subscribe online at www.conciliumjournal.co.uk

Please enter my annual subscription for Concilium starting with issue 2020/3.

Individuals
____ £52 UK
____ £75 overseas and (Euro €92, US $110)

Institutions
____ £75 UK
____ £95 overseas and (Euro €120, US $145)

Postage included – airmail for overseas subscribers

Payment Details:
Payment can be made by cheque (£ Sterling only), by credit/debit card or bank transfer.
a. I enclose a cheque for £ _____ Payable to Hymns Ancient and Modern Ltd
b. To pay by Visa/Mastercard please contact us on +44(0)1603 785911 or go to www.conciliumjournal.co.uk
c. To pay in US $ or Euro € by bank transfer please contact us on +44(0)1603 785911

Contact Details:
Name ....
Address ....
....
Telephone .... E-mail ....

Send your order to *Concilium*, **Hymns Ancient and Modern Ltd**
13a Hellesdon Park Road, Norwich NR6 5DR, UK
E-mail: concilium@hymnsam.co.uk
or order online at www.conciliumjournal.co.uk

Customer service information
All orders must be prepaid. Your subscription will begin with the next issue of Concilium. If you have any queries or require Information about other payment methods, please contact our Customer Services department.

www.ingramcontent.com/pod-product-compliance
Ingram Content Group UK Ltd.
Pitfield, Milton Keynes, MK11 3LW, UK
UKHW042006230426
12048UKWH00009B/590